Breastfeeding
Pure & Simple

Breastfeeding
Pure & Simple

Gwen Gotsch

La Leche League International
Franklin Park, Illinois

January 1994
© 1993 La Leche League International
Cover photo, cover design, and book design,
    David C. Arendt
Printed in the USA
All Rights Reserved
Library of Congress 93-080164
ISBN 0-912500-42-5

This book is dedicated to the staff, present and past, at La Leche League International Headquarters; people whose commitment to helping mothers and babies has made a difference in the lives of families around the world.

Contents

Acknowledgements

This book is based on the experiences of many thousands of women who have shared their breastfeeding stories with each other in the years since La Leche League's founding in 1956. They have helped to build a tradition of breastfeeding knowledge from which families all over the world benefit. My special thanks go to the following individuals who worked on this book: David Arendt for the design and and for his patience in taking photographs; Kim Cavaliero for the title; Bill Sears, Jan Riordan, Betty Crase, and Marijane McEwan, for reading the manuscript; Elayne Shpak for typing; Lon Grahnke for perspectives on fathering; and Judy Torgus, who came up with the idea for this book, asked me to write it, and nagged me cheerfully until it was finished.

Gwen Gotsch

Photo Credits

David Arendt, front cover, pages 1, 3, 9, 11, 13, 25, 26, 27, 28, 29, 30, 31, 32, 48, 59, 62, 65, 69, 73, 75, 78, 79, 81, 82, 85, 89, 94, 101

JJ Anderson, pages 5, 90, 105, 107

Mary Ann Cahill, page 7

Medela, Inc., page 14

Darrell Rideout, page 17, 21

Mary Joan Deutschbein, page 23

Judy Torgus, pages 19, 37

Dariuz Michalowski, page 35

Jean Hoelscher, Association for Breastfeeding Fashions, pages 41, 83, 103

Paul Torgus, page 44, (Sketches)

Cindi Salazar, pages 45, 66

Pascale, page 54

Dale Pfeiffer, page 93

Eleanor Randall, page 70

Sharon Kay, page 72

Lon Grahnke, page 99, back cover

Foreword

Twenty-five years ago I knew little about breastfeeding, and I didn't think it made much difference. In medical school the baby feeding lectures were mainly recitations of the contents of the formula can. I was fresh out of school and into pediatric practice when my first breastfeeding patient told me she hadn't experienced a let-down yet; I thought she meant postpartum depression. Now, after twenty years of pediatric practice and being in the supporting role as my wife, Martha, breastfed all eight of our children, I am happy to report: breastfeeding does matter.

There will be times when mothers feel that breastfeeding is all giving, giving, giving. This is true early on in the breastfeeding relationship. Babies are takers, and parents are givers. But in our breastfeeding experience we have learned to appreciate the concept of mutual giving—the more you give to your baby, the more the baby gives back to you. When a mother breastfeeds her baby, she gives nourishment and comfort. The baby's sucking, in turn, stimulates the release of hormones that further enhance mothering behavior.

Another dividend to expect is mutual sensitivity. Breastfeeding helps you become more sensitive to your baby and helps your baby become more sensitive to you. This sensitivity helps breastfeeding mothers make the right choice at the right time when confronted with the daily "What do I do now?" baby-care decisions. The connected pair mirror each other's feelings. Baby learns about himself through mother's eyes. The mother reflects the baby's value to her, and therefore to himself. Breastfeeding helps mothers click into these feelings earlier and maintain them longer.

Everything a breastfeeding mother needs to know is concisely found in BREASTFEEDING *Pure & Simple*. This little book with lots of information will help newborns and new mothers get connected and stay connected. As an author myself, I truly enjoyed how Gwen Gotsch has masterfully presented so much information in so few pages. This book is indeed a testimony to the axiom, "Good things come in small packages."

Both novice breastfeeding mothers and professionals who offer breastfeeding advice will find this book a pleasure to read and a valuable lactation resource.

William Sears, MD
Clinical Assistant Professor of Pediatrics
University of Southern California
School of Medicine

Chapter One

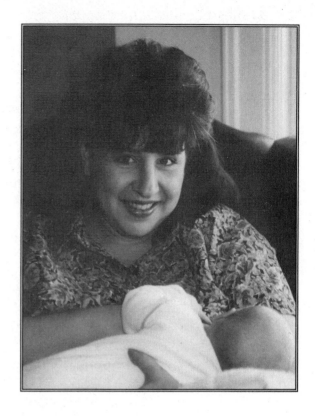

Breastfeeding in Today's World

Mothers agree, it's worth it.

Breastfeeding your baby requires some effort, but it definitely has its rewards. A healthy, thriving baby is one of the payoffs; a real sense of accomplishment for mother is another. Many a breastfeeding mother over the years has paused to gaze at her bright-eyed three- or four-month-old nursling, so much bigger now than at birth, and smiled proudly to herself while thinking, "I did that. My body nourished that baby."

Breastfeeding makes sense—human milk is the perfect food for babies. It contains all the nutrition babies need, along with protection from infection and disease. It comes from the same warm maternal body that nourishes the baby in the womb, holds and soothes the newborn in tender embraces, and helps the growing infant feel secure while getting to know an exciting but sometimes overwhelming new world. Mother's milk is there, warm and sweet and waiting, in response to baby's need for food and comfort.

Breastfeeding is not all romance. It may be natural, but breastfeeding a baby, like mothering, is an art, a skill that requires learning and practice. The mother and baby teach each other during the first days and weeks, and more discoveries follow as the months go by. Some lessons are learned quickly. Others take a little longer. Problems are solved more easily within a supportive environment; nevertheless, many mothers breastfeed successfully on their own.

This book is an introduction to the art of breastfeeding. It tells you what you need to know to get off to a good start and to continue nursing your baby through the first several months of life. It also tells you something about feelings that go along with breastfeeding and how to overcome common problems. With support and accurate information, breastfeeding can be a happy, treasured experience for both baby and mother.

Why mothers breastfeed

For many families, breastfeeding is the natural thing to do; they prefer an "all natural" product over one concocted in a factory. Human milk has been tested by time over thousands of years, and its special properties cannot be duplicated by infant formula. Babies who are breastfed have significant nutritional, immunological, and psychological advantages.

Human milk is the nutritional standard against which infant formula is measured, but it has properties that make it far superior. The composition of human milk is always changing to meet the changing needs of the developing infant. The first milk, a thick yellowish substance called colostrum, is high in protein, low in fat, and contains a high concentration of immune factors, which may be especially important to the baby in the first days of life outside the womb. As the mother's breasts begin to make more milk, the concentrations of protein and immune factors gradually decrease and levels of fat, lactose, and total calories increase. As the baby gets older, milk composition varies less, but it will change again during weaning. One study found that an older baby, who is nursing more for comfort than nutrition, receives a greater concentration of immune factors; breastfeeding continues to play a role in protecting the weaning child from disease.

Breastfeeding protects against infection

The list of protective factors in human milk is a long one, and scientists are only beginning to unravel the mysteries of how they all work together to protect the baby from infection. Meanwhile, studies comparing groups of breastfed and formula-fed babies clearly show that breastfed babies have fewer and less severe problems with diarrhea, respiratory infections, ear infections, and other common diseases. Breastfed babies are much less likely to end up in the hospital with a serious illness. They are also less likely to become victims of Sudden Infant Death Syndrome (SIDS).

Each mother's milk helps to protect her baby from whatever illness is going around.

One especially interesting feature of breastfeeding's immunological benefits is the way each mother's milk helps to protect her baby from whatever illness is going around. When the mother is exposed to bacteria or a virus, her more mature immune system quickly produces antibodies that are transferred to the baby through the milk. This is important, because young infants cannot muster the same level of defense against infection as adults. It's also a reminder to breastfeeding mothers and those who advise them: if a mother is feeling ill, coming down with a cold or flu, she should not stop nursing or even hesitate to breastfeed her baby. Her milk will not harm her baby; in fact, it will help the baby fight off the infection.

Human milk provides ideal nutrition

Breastfed babies generally need to be fed more often than formula-fed babies. One reason for this is that human milk is very well suited to the baby's digestive system and is digested very quickly. The protein is made up of 60 percent whey proteins and 40 percent casein proteins; this makes a very soft curd that is easy and efficient to digest. (Cow's milk contains only 20 percent whey proteins and 80 percent casein.) The fat in human milk is also highly digestible because of the enzyme lipase, which keeps the fat globules small and totally digestible. Since fat is the major source of energy for infants, its easy availability is important to growth.

Besides fat and protein, the other major components of human milk are water and lactose, or milk sugar. Levels of lactose are higher in species with bigger brains, so it's not surprising that human milk contains more lactose than cow's milk. It is important for newborn growth, central nervous system development, and the absorption of calcium. Human milk provides all the water that infants need. Even in very warm, dry climates, breastfed babies do not need supplementary bottles of water.

Human milk provides all the nutrients that infants need.

All the vitamins, minerals, and trace elements that babies need to grow, develop, and stay healthy can be found in human milk. Iron levels are low, as in all mammal milk, but the iron is absorbed and used far more efficiently than that in iron-fortified formula. Breastfed babies do not need iron supplements. Human milk's higher potassium levels and low sodium levels may help protect against the development of high blood pressure. And the vitamins in human milk meet all of baby's needs. Some physicians recommend vitamin D supplements for breastfed babies, but even these are not usually necessary for most mothers and babies.

Science is just beginning to investigate the effects of various enzymes and hormones in human milk on the development of the baby. Some of these aid infant digestion, others have a role in killing bacteria. Hormones from human milk help to regulate newborns' biochemical responses to feedings and promote the growth and development of the intestinal tract. These highly specialized functions cannot be duplicated by infant formula.

Breastfeeding brings mother and baby closer together

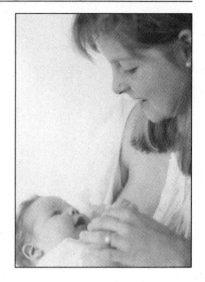

Breastfeeding is an undeniably different experience from bottle-feeding. The breastfed baby is pulled close against the mother, touching her warm, smooth skin. The nipple is soft and pliable; it is shaped by baby's mouth. The baby sucks at his own rate, and the sucking determines how fast the milk flows and when the feeding is over. A hungry baby will suck eagerly until his tummy is full. A baby who is upset may suck more for comfort, and the small amounts of milk he receives, plus the rhythm of his suck, will lull him into a more peaceful state. Whether mother is gazing into baby's eyes or talking, reading, or watching television during a feeding, her body is actively present for her baby. Feeding is always associated with the warmth and security that is mother.

Breastfed babies make their mothers feel special.

Babies let their mothers know how much they enjoy nursing: they wriggle with delight, they smile, they coo, they play games, they fall blissfully asleep. They make their mothers feel important, special, and capable. Frequent nursing sessions, following the baby's cues, help mothers learn to understand their baby's behavior and become flexible about meeting baby's needs. Prolactin and oxytocin, the hormones that regulate milk production and release, also produce feelings of calm, relaxation, and love. Both baby and mother benefit from the feelings of closeness that come from breastfeeding.

Breastfeeding is practical

Breastfeeding is also cheap, convenient, and good for the environment. It costs $20 to $30 a week to buy infant formula in the United States, but human milk is free, and available from mother instantly anywhere. With breastfeeding, there's no need to mix formula or worry about how many bottles to bring along on an outing, how to keep them cold, or how to warm them when you need them. Human milk doesn't pollute the environment—its production and distribution systems don't require electrical energy, throwaway packaging, cross-country shipping, or cows that produce excess methane gas.

Breastfeeding gives busy mothers many chances during the day to sit down and rest for a while, or to read books or play games with baby's older sibling. Nighttime feedings are simple, and nursing will often put mother as well as baby back to sleep quickly. While critics of breastfeeding like to point out that breastfeeding is "inconvenient" or "difficult in today's busy world," experienced breastfeeding mothers often feel that the best thing about breastfeeding is its simplicity and convenience.

Confidence: What breastfeeding mothers need most

Breastfeeding involves a mother's heart and mind as well as her body, and gaining confidence is an important part of learning to nurse her baby. But sometimes confidence in breastfeeding can be hard to come by.

Several generations ago mothers didn't turn to books for advice about breastfeeding. They learned about nursing their babies from seeing other women breastfeed healthy, thriving infants, and they learned from other women's problems, too. Almost everybody breastfed, because babies who were "hand-fed" on animal milk or other concoctions often didn't survive.

Today, fortunately, artificial feeding is not so dangerous, as long as a mother has access to clean water, fuel, and affordable supplies of infant formula (conditions that are difficult to meet in many parts of the world). But even though human milk remains the standard for infant feeding, artificial feeding has become a common and well-established part of today's baby culture. The decorations, cards, and wrappings at baby showers picture bottles along with all the other

equipment every baby "requires." Infant formula is advertised on television, and breastfeeding women find coupons for formula in their mailbox, right about the time when babies experience growth spurts and mothers may have doubts about their milk supply. Hospitals may even send formula samples home with breastfeeding mothers—implying that breastfeeding may not succeed. Is it any wonder that new mothers have doubts and anxieties about breastfeeding?

Breastfeeding really does work, and in most circumstances, it's surprisingly simple. Confidence in breastfeeding will come with experience. However, most of today's soon-to-be mothers were not breastfed as babies, and unless they have friends who are nursing babies, they may never have gotten a close look at a baby latched onto a breast and actively sucking. But there are ways to gain experience with breastfeeding before your baby is born. Learning about breastfeeding, seeking out health-care providers who have confidence in breastfeeding, and talking to experienced, successful nursing mothers will help a mother gain confidence in her ability to breastfeed her baby.

Breastfeeding is not difficult or complicated, but it does take some practice for mothers and babies to become skilled at it. The problems that women sometimes encounter with breastfeeding can be solved, and deserve to be. Most of them are not medical problems at all, but are the result of misunderstanding the needs of mothers and babies. The answer to breastfeeding problems is seldom a bottle of formula; the best solution is the telephone—a call to someone knowledgeable about breastfeeding.

La Leche League International

La Leche League offers the kind of support that many women feel is essential to breastfeeding success. For more than thirty-five years, La Leche League has been learning about breastfeeding from mothers and the people who assist them and has been sharing this knowledge with other mothers and with health professionals all over the world. La Leche League's mother-to-mother support and its practical approach to parenting have enabled millions of women to enjoy breastfeeding and mothering their babies.

Problems that women encounter with breastfeeding deserve to be solved.

La Leche League Leaders are available by phone to answer questions about breastfeeding. They are all experienced nursing mothers who have been accredited by La Leche League International. Written materials, workshops, conferences, and networking with other Leaders have prepared them to give you the information you need, to help you explore options for solving problems, and to offer the encouraging words you need to hear. If you have a breastfeeding question a La Leche League Leader can't answer herself, she can use LLLI's vast network of resources to find out what you need to know. From fussy babies, critical relatives, and dwindling milk supplies to going back to work or needing to take medication, breastfeeding dilemmas are La Leche League's business.

Local La Leche League Groups offer monthly meetings at which expectant and new mothers gather along with experienced breastfeeding mothers and the Group's Leaders. They discuss the how-to's, the whys, the what-not-to-do's of breastfeeding and talk of their own experiences. Mothers can speak frankly about difficulties they're having with nursing or with the day-to-day stresses of motherhood. They can be assured of responses that are not only full of helpful ideas but are also warmly supportive of every mother's efforts to do the very best for her own baby and family.

To find a La Leche League Group in your area, call La Leche League International Headquarters at 1-800-LA LECHE or 708-455-7730. The staff there can provide you with names and phone numbers of La Leche League Leaders near you. They'll also be happy to send you an LLLI Catalogue and other information. You may also find information about La Leche League meetings listed in your local newspaper or posted in your doctor's office, or your childbirth educator may be able to refer you to a local LLL Group.

At La Leche League meetings you find mothers helping other mothers with information and confidence-building support.

Support is crucial to new mothers. Your partner, your friends, your family will play important roles, caring for you and encouraging you as you learn to breastfeed and mother your baby. La Leche League can provide an added boost, especially if you should run into an unusualproblem or if the people closest to you understand little about breastfeeding.

Chapter Two

Getting Ready

All through pregnancy, a woman's body prepares for breastfeeding.

Her breasts enlarge and may feel tender as the milk-making structures inside of them grow. The areola, the pigmented area around the nipple, darkens, and the nipples may become more erect and protruding. The Montgomery's glands, the pimply bumps around the nipple, secrete a substance that lubricates the nipples and protects them. Sometime in the second trimester, the breasts begin producing colostrum, the first milk that is especially high in antibodies. Some women notice small amounts of colostrum leaking from their breasts late in pregnancy.

All these changes take place whether or not a mother plans to breastfeed. So the most important part of getting ready to breastfeed is done naturally and automatically. And really, beyond this, little preparation is needed.

However, adding a new baby to your life is a big change and a challenge. Knowing what to expect and being prepared can ease the way.

Breast and nipple care

As you look ahead to breastfeeding, you may begin to think of your breasts in a new way. From the time when a girl's figure changes to that of a woman's, breasts are an important part of her body image and her feminine identity. Some women like their breasts and some don't; some are comfortable handling them and others aren't. Some women are anxious about breastfeeding while others feel more confident.

Thinking of breasts as functioning organs, a source of nourishment and nurture for an infant, can seem odd, even scary, at first. Women wonder if their breasts will make enough milk, how the baby will get the milk out of there, and whether their breasts, changed by pregnancy, will ever be the same again. Discovering after the baby is born that the whole process really does work can be an awesome experience, one that gives a woman a new appreciation of her body and her breasts.

Breasts and nipples come in many sizes and shapes. Breast size has no effect on a woman's ability to produce milk for her baby. Small breasts contain plenty of milk-producing glands; larger breasts contain more fatty tissue—which has no influence on lactation.

Buying bras

Whether or not to wear a bra is up to you. Some women are more comfortable without one. Pregnancy alters the size, shape, and firmness of breasts, regardless of whether or not a woman goes on to breastfeed. Heredity and gravity influence breast contours far more than wearing or not wearing a bra.

You'll probably find that you need a larger bra size during pregnancy. It makes sense to buy bras with cups that open so you can use them later when you're nursing. You may need bras that are larger still during the first weeks after your baby is born. Shop for nursing bras during the last few weeks of pregnancy, but buy only two or three at first. If you find a particular style comfortable, you can get more later. There should be extra room in the cup and an extra row of hooks in the back to allow for breast enlargement. The fastener on the cup should be easy to open and close with one hand, while the other arm holds the baby. Bras should be comfortable; they shouldn't pinch or bind. Be especially careful with underwires, which can obstruct the flow of milk if they don't fit properly.

Bras and breast pads (used by some women to absorb milk leakage) should allow air to circulate to the nipples. This helps prevent chapping and soreness. All-cotton materials are best; avoid bras and pads with plastic linings.

Breast surgery

Previous breast surgery can affect breastfeeding if milk ducts or major nerves have been severed. In some types of breast reduction surgery, the ducts are cut; this can prevent the milk from reaching the nipple during breastfeeding. Breast implants themselves don't usually present problems for breastfeeding, but sometimes nerves or ducts are cut during breast augmentation surgery. Checking with the surgeon can help clarify exactly what was done, but the only way to find out for sure if breastfeeding will work in a given situation is to go ahead and give it a try, paying close attention to the basics: positioning and latch-on, signs that the baby is getting enough milk, and frequent feedings.

Nipple preparation

Years ago, doctors, nurses, and even breastfeeding advocates prescribed all kinds of regimens to help pregnant women "toughen" their nipples ahead of time, in order to avoid soreness during breastfeeding. Happily, those days are gone. Experts now agree that most sore

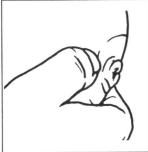

To check for inverted nipples, compress the areola an inch behind the base of the nipple. It should protrude rather than cave in.

Breast shells can correct inverted nipples.

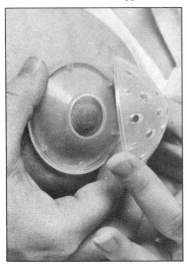

nipples are the result of babies being poorly positioned at the breast during feedings or not sucking effectively, and that you really can't toughen up a nipple anyway. Nipples are supposed to be pliable and sensitive.

Most mothers don't need to do anything special to prepare their nipples for breastfeeding. Pregnant and nursing women should avoid using soap on their nipples—you don't want to wash away the natural oils that keep the skin supple. It isn't necessary, but it won't hurt to use a lotion or moisturizer on the nipples, as long as it's applied sparingly. Modified lanolin (sold under the brand name of Lansinoh®) is a good choice and can also be used after the baby arrives.

Inverted nipples

Flat or inverted nipples can make latching- on to the breast more difficult for the baby; babies usually find it easier to grasp a nipple that protrudes from the breast. Checking for inverted nipples during pregnancy is important; treating them before the baby is born may prevent a great deal of frustration during the first weeks of breastfeeding.

To determine if your nipples are flat or inverted, gently compress the areola about an inch behind the base of the nipple. A flat nipple cannot be compressed outward and does not protrude when stimulated. An inverted nipple caves in when the areola is compressed. Your nipples are not identical; a woman may have one nipple that is very inverted while the other may be only slightly inverted or have no problem at all.

Nipples invert because tiny bands of tissue connect them to the inside of the breast. Treatment for inverted or flat nipples stretches these bands, enabling the nipple to protrude.

One way to treat inverted nipples is to use breast shells. These hard, lightweight plastic cups are worn inside a bra. An inner ring, worn next to the skin, applies gentle pressure on the areola, causing the nipple to protrude through the center. The outer cup holds the bra away from the nipple, for comfort. You wear the breast shells for a few hours a day at first and gradually increase the time you use them. After the baby is born, the shells can be worn before feedings to help the nipple protrude. Breast shells are also called breast shields, milk cups, breast cups, or Woolwich shields. Wearing them may seem peculiar at first, but they are not noticeable under clothing.

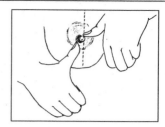

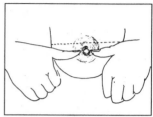

The Hoffman technique has also been used to draw out the flat or inverted nipples. To do this, place your thumbs on either side of the base of the nipple. Press in firmly against the breast and at the same time, pull the thumbs away from each other. Move the thumbs around the base of the nipple to a new position and repeat. Do this several times a day. Once the nipple begins to protrude, nipple rolls may also be helpful. Grasp the nipple at its base between the thumb and the index finger. Press the fingers together and gently pull the nipple out, turning it up and then down.

The Hoffman Technique.

Inverted nipples need not prevent a mother from breastfeeding, even if she does nothing about them during her pregnancy. Careful attention to how the baby is positioned at the breast and lots of opportunities for practice enable most full-term healthy babies to latch on to the breast and draw out the nipple with their sucking.

Inverted nipples need not prevent a mother from breastfeeding.

If you have questions about inverted nipples, or if you're not sure if you have inverted nipples, talk to a La Leche League Leader, health care provider, doctor, or midwife with some knowledge of breastfeeding. Many professionals who provide health care for pregnant women routinely check for inverted nipples when doing breast exams. If you have questions about breastfeeding with inverted nipples, talk to a La Leche League Leader. She can help you anticipate difficulties and prepare for a good start with breastfeeding. A La Leche League Leader can also tell you where to purchase breast shells in your community.

Nipple Rolls

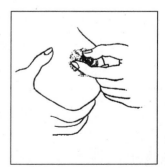

Choosing health-care providers

Most doctors nowadays go along with the maxim that "breast is best," but not all of them have learned enough about breastfeeding to be helpful to nursing mothers. Most physicians—even pediatricians—are taught little or nothing about breastfeeding techniques in the classroom or lecture hall. Those who do know the ins and outs of breastfeeding have learned on the job, from watching other knowledgeable health workers, from talking to experienced nursing mothers, or from nursing their own babies.

Physicians who are knowledgeable and enthusiastic about breastfeeding are a blessing to nursing mothers. They help them off to a good start and encourage them to continue. Hospitals with "baby-friendly" routines also make a difference. Studies have shown that breastfeeding rates vary greatly, depending on the hospital staff's attitude toward breastfeeding.

Choosing health-care providers may seem like a daunting task, and the number of eligible candidates may be limited by things beyond your control—for example, geography or the provisions of your health insurance plan. Still, making inquiries, interviewing, and stating your needs ahead of time will help you establish a good relationship with your physician, one that may be very important in the months to come.

There are many ways to find a doctor who suits your needs. Ask around—most people are happy to tell you about their physician. Talking to other mothers at La Leche League meetings is one way to find out about doctors who are supportive of breastfeeding. Calls to local hospitals or area medical societies will also yield names. Your obstetrician or midwife may be able to recommend colleagues who are supportive of breastfeeding.

To find out more about a doctor, call his or her office. The staff there can answer basic questions about office hours, procedures for calling after hours, back-up, professional credentials, hospital affiliation, insurance, and fees. When you've narrowed down the field to just a few names, call and make an appointment to talk with the doctor. Some physicians will give you a free consultation; others may charge a fee.

Make a list of questions to ask at the interview. Don't expect to get them all into the conversation. More important than covering every possible contingency is finding someone with whom you can communicate, who shows genuine respect and interest in your needs and choices, and whose basic philosophy of child-bearing and child- rearing is compatible with yours. Finding a physician who is flexible and willing to work with you to solve a problem is more important than finding one who knows all the "right" answers.

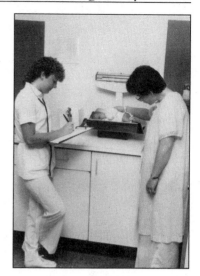

Baby doctors

Pediatricians and many family physicians care for infants and children. Besides being available in case of serious illness, they provide well-baby checkups, immunizations, reassurance, and answers to questions about everything from sniffles and rashes to infant behavior, development, and parenting skills.

Look for a physician who shows genuine respect for your choices.

When interviewing potential doctors for your baby, you'll want to inquire about their feelings about breastfeeding. However, it's more important to ask what percentage of babies in the practice are breastfed, and for how long. How many mothers use supplements? When and how does the physician recommend weaning? Were the doctor's own children breastfed? What will the doctor do to help you get off to a good start at breastfeeding in the first days after birth? Following up with these kinds of questions will reveal more about a physician's support for nursing mothers than a simple "How do you feel about breastfeeding?" Ask also about office staff, since you may have as much contact with these people as with the doctor. Do any staff members have a special interest in helping nursing mothers? What are their qualifications and experience?

You may find a supportive, knowledgeable physician on the first try, or you may not find such a creature at all in your community. Let your doctor know what you need and why. Remember that many physicians have learned about breastfeeding from mothers in their practices. Your enthusiasm and knowledge about breastfeeding may rub off on your doctor.

Hospital and birth attendants

In the first 24 to 48 hours after the birth of a baby, hospital routines loom large in the day and nighttime life of a nursing mother. Breastfeeding gets off to the best start when mother and baby can be together early and often, preferably all the time. New babies need to nurse frequently, but at unpredictable intervals. This is easier to do in hospitals where the baby stays with the mother 24 hours a day or when mother and baby return home soon after the birth. Rules and routines that keep mother in one room and baby in the nursery for specified times of the day interfere with the natural rhythms of breastfeeding and with the mother and baby getting to know one another.

Ideally, hospital staff will not only allow, but also encourage a breastfeeding mother to keep her baby at her side and nurse frequently, following the baby's cues. Keeping baby close also guards against the possibility that nursery staff will give the baby bottles of formula or water or offer a pacifier, all of which can interfere with breastfeeding.

To learn more about a hospital's policies, call and arrange to talk with the head nurse of the birth and postpartum unit. Besides telling you about hospital routines, she may also be able to identify which of the physicians on staff share your views on birth and are supportive of breastfeeding. Tours or open houses at hospitals or birth centers are another source of information about facilities, routines, and breastfeeding policies.

Breastfeeding women benefit from positive experiences with labor and birth; the feeling that you've managed well and have been treated with respect during the challenges of birthing carries over into your self-confidence as a mother. While some difficult situations call for all the medical help that modern obstetrics can muster, much of the technology associated with birth in the hospital can hinder a mother in her efforts to give birth naturally. And many of the medications given to mothers in labor and delivery alter infant sucking behavior for several days after birth.

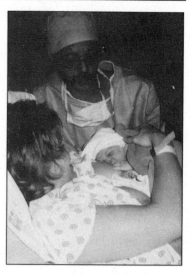

Learn about birth, medical interventions, and ways to cope with contractions by taking childbirth education classes and by reading a variety of books. (The bibliography at the end of this book lists several books on pregnancy and birth.) Discuss your plans for the birth with your care provider. Sometimes it's a good idea to put it all down in writing and ask the doctor to sign the birth plan. You can then take copies to the hospital and refer staff members to your agreement with your doctor if they propose to do something you don't want. You might also want to get orders ahead of time from your baby's doctor, specifying that your baby is to be breastfed frequently and is not to be given formula or water in the nursery.

Of course, you don't have to have a "perfect" birth for breastfeeding to succeed. Breastfeeding will work, even if there are unforeseen complications or you have a cesarean or you and your baby are separated for a time after birth. You can't control everything that happens, even under the best of circumstances. But you can know that once your baby is in your arms, you are just exactly what he needs.

Adjusting your lifestyle

After your baby arrives, you'll be spending lots of time with him, holding him, rocking him, nursing him. Prenatal visions of spotless housekeeping, time for hobbies, and gourmet cooking, all accomplished while the baby takes long naps, will fade into the reality of full-time baby care. There may not be much time for anything else. Life will settle into manageable routines eventually, but the first weeks postpartum go by in a blur for many new families.

Anticipating your after-baby needs can smooth the

transition from one way of life to another. Don't plan on tackling big projects during your baby's first months. If there's heavy cleaning or a decorating project that needs attention, volunteer efforts that demand your time, or a job-related deadline that must be met, plan on getting the work done well ahead of your due date. Give yourself the luxury of devoting as much attention as you desire to your new baby. Stock up on groceries, and cook and freeze meals ahead of time. Clean closets, and give some thought to what you can wear in those first weeks after birth, when your waistline is not yet back to normal and two-piece outfits are handiest for nursing.

If parents, in-laws, or friends offer to help in the days and weeks postpartum, ask them to see to it that you and your family are fed and have clean clothes and a relatively neat environment. Let them know that what you'll need the most is someone to take care of you so that you can take care of and get to know your baby. Tell potential helpers about your plans to breastfeed, and let them know that their support is important to you.

Your helpers should take care of you so that you can care for the baby.

Returning to work

Employers, understandably, want to know if and when mothers will be returning to work after their babies are born. Although it takes some determination, you can continue to breastfeed even if you and your baby are separated during an eight-hour workday. Both you and your baby will benefit, however, from as much time off as possible after the birth, to allow breastfeeding to become well established and to get to know one another.

The strength of your feeling for your baby after he's born may surprise you. Leaving him with a substitute caregiver will be difficult—for you and for him. Babies need their mother's continuing presence to develop to their fullest potential.

If possible, it's wise not to make a firm commitment about your return to work until after the baby is born. After you've had a chance to adjust to being his mother, you can shape your plans according to your baby's needs. Studies have found that part-time

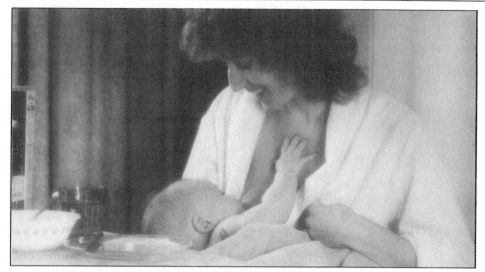

employment is more conducive to continued breastfeeding than working 40 hours a week, and that delaying the return to work by several months also makes breastfeeding easier.

If full-time mothering is possible for you (or you and your partner can find a way to make it possible), give that choice serious consideration. Many psychologists believe that a secure attachment between mother and baby is critical to the child's self-image and ability to form relationships later on. (See the bibliography at the end of the book for more on this subject.)

Staying home

For many women, having their first baby, or sometimes their second, marks a transition into being at home full-time, after having worked for a number of years. Even when you've looked forward to enjoying full-time mothering, the adjustment will take time. Your new lifestyle will bring new demands, a need to find ways of managing your time, even the need to make new friends. Whether your time at home is a maternity leave or the beginning of a new life as a full-time mother, build in plans for taking care of yourself. The quiet moments of rest that come with breastfeeding will help you to find time to read, enjoy some television, converse with your family and friends, or just think and dream. This special time will never come again. Enjoy.

Chapter Three

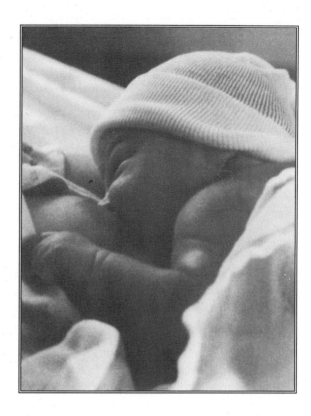

Off to a
Good Start

First breastfeedings are wonderful, exciting, and sometimes a bit awkward.

      Babies know a lot about nursing right from the start. Even so, they need some guidance from their mothers—who are learning themselves. Some babies nurse like pros at the very beginning; others may be more tentative in the first few days. You may feel clumsy or inexperienced during these initial feedings, but you and your baby will soon get accustomed to each other.

Newborns, new mothers, and nursing

Babies are born with reflexes that help them learn to feed at the breast. Touch their cheeks and they turn their heads, searching for a nipple. Their mouths open wide, ready to grasp the breast, and once they have latched on, they suck and swallow readily. They even know when their tummies are full and it's time to let go.

Mothers' bodies also react by reflex. Once the placenta is delivered, levels of estrogen and progesterone fall, allowing the hormone prolactin to stimulate plentiful milk production in the breasts within two or three days. This is often referred to as the milk "coming in," and can be quite dramatic. From this point on, the law of supply and demand regulates milk production: the more the baby sucks and the more milk that is removed from the breast, the more milk the mother's body will make.

When the baby is put to the breast, the mother's system releases another hormone, oxytocin, which causes tiny muscles to squeeze the milk out of the cells high in the breast where it is made, forcing it down the milk ducts toward the nipple. This is called the milk-ejection reflex or the let-down. Oxytocin also causes the uterus to contract, helping it return to its non-pregnant size more quickly. These contractions, while beneficial, may be noticeably uncomfortable for a few days, especially with second or subsequent births. Do some deep breathing or try another relaxation technique if these "afterpains" trouble you. You might also talk to your doctor or midwife about using a non-aspirin pain reliever.

Breastfeeding soon after birth

A newborn's first hour or so after birth is spent in quiet alertness, a state where her body is calm and all her energy is focused on seeing and hearing. Newborns in the quiet alert state gaze into adult faces and respond to their mother's voice, already deeply familiar to them from the months spent inside her body. This special time should not be wasted on hospital routines that separate

babies from parents. Unless there is a problem requiring immediate attention, newborn babies belong with their mothers. Eyedrops (which temporarily blur infant vision), baths, and exams can wait until parents and baby have had time to become acquainted. Mother's body will keep baby warm, and medical personnel can observe mother and baby without coming between them.

Mothers and babies are often ready to nurse soon after birth, during those magical moments when mother holds the tiny infant who has just emerged from her body. A newborn baby placed on her mother's chest, skin-to-skin, will seek the nipple, nuzzle it, lick it, and very likely latch on and suck. These first attempts at breastfeeding soothe newborns and warm them. They also reassure mothers and help control postpartum bleeding, thanks to the effects of oxytocin on the uterus.

Your partner or one of your care providers can lend a hand with these first attempts at nursing. You may need help getting the baby in a comfortable position at the breast. Don't worry too much about getting everything just perfect at first. Now is a time to relax and enjoy your baby after the hard work of giving birth.

A newborn baby will seek the nipple, latch on, and suck.

Some babies may not be interested in breastfeeding at this time; they may be preoccupied with all the new sensations of life outside the womb. In some cases, mother and baby may be too tired from the work of the delivery; after both have had a good rest they will be ready to begin nursing.

Talk to your birth attendant ahead of time about keeping baby close to you in the first hours after birth and about breastfeeding then. Even if you have a cesarean, it should still be possible for you to share some or all of this special time with your baby.

Getting baby started at the breast

You and your baby will get lots of practice at breastfeeding in the first weeks after birth. It's important to get it right. Expert breastfeeders—babies of five or six

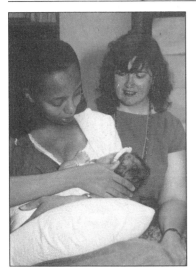

These mothers are using pillows to bring their babies up to the level of their breasts.

Their babies are lying on their sides, tummy to tummy with their mothers, pulled in close for breastfeeding.

months of age—can nurse efficiently in just about any position, even while wriggling around. But at first, while your baby is learning what to do, you will need to pay careful attention. How you are sitting or lying, how you hold your baby, and how you offer the breast all affect the position of the baby's mouth on the breast as she nurses. Not getting latched on properly can lead to sore nipples for mother, poor weight gain for baby, and frustration for everyone.

Early breastfeedings work best if the baby is alert and calm. Take a few minutes to soothe a fussy baby or wake a sleepy one before you offer the breast.

To wake a sleepy baby gently, lay her along your forearms, facing you at a right angle to your body, and slowly bring her to a more upright position. You can repeat this up-and-down motion while you talk to her and call her name. When she opens her eyes, try to get her to look at you; dim the lights so that she can keep her eyes open comfortably. If the room is not cold or drafty, undress her down to her diaper. Babies nurse better when they are not too warm, and skin-to-skin contact with mother is very stimulating. A lightweight receiving blanket tucked around both of you will keep her cozy.

Positioning the baby

When you and your baby are ready to nurse, the first thing to do is make sure that you are comfortable. Use pillows to support your back so that you can sit up straight or lean back at a slight angle. Place one or two pillows on your lap to bring the baby's mouth up to the level of your nipple. A pillow can also help support your elbow. You should not have to lean over your baby to nurse her, nor should you be leaning way back. It's usually easier to breastfeed in a straight, comfortable chair with arms than sitting up in a hospital bed. If you're not very tall, a footstool or a few big books under your feet can help you sit straighter and more comfortably. If you're sitting in bed, bend your knees and support them with a pillow to help straighten your back and shoulders.

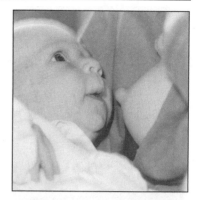

Hold your baby on her side, her head at the inside of your elbow, her neck and shoulders supported along your forearm, and your hand at her buttocks. Her head, neck, and body should be in a straight line. Pull her in close; you and she should be tummy-to-tummy. Your baby should not have to turn her head to take the breast. (It's very hard to swallow with your head turned sideways—try it!) Her bottom arm can nestle into your abdomen, or extend back around your waist, whichever is more comfortable.

Hold your breast with your hand in the shape of a C, fingers underneath, thumb on top, well back from the areola. Cup your breast gently, don't squeeze and distort its shape. If you have large breasts, try using a rolled-up towel or receiving blanket underneath to help support the breast. If your breasts are small, you may not need to support them at all once the feeding is underway.

Latching on and sucking

Tickle the baby's lips lightly with your nipple to encourage her to open wide. As she opens her mouth wide, quickly pull her in close to take the breast. The nipple should be far back in her mouth, and she should take at least an inch of the areola as well. The tip of her nose should be touching the breast. Even when pulled in this close, she will not have trouble breathing; babies' noses are turned up and their nostrils flare out just so they can breathe while breastfeeding. The baby's chin should also touch the breast, and her lips should be flanged outward.

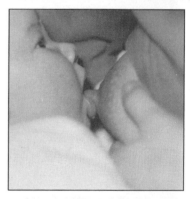

Proper positioning of the baby at the breast and the baby's mouth on the breast help her to compress the milk ducts under the areola and obtain the most milk. Good positioning also protects mother's nipple. Breastfeeding should not hurt. Sore nipples are caused by friction—the baby's tongue or gums rubbing the sensitive skin of the nipple during sucking. If the nipple is far enough back in the baby's mouth, it is away from all the movement that can cause damage.

*Say "Open" to encourage your baby
to open her mouth wide
like a yawn.*

Problems? Try again

Don't worry if your baby doesn't latch on at the first try. Stay calm, and try again. If the baby is sucking only on the end of the nipple, press down a bit on the breast tissue or put your finger into the corner of the baby's mouth to break the suction and take the baby off. Check the baby's position and yours, and then offer the breast again. Don't let the baby suck only on the nipple—you'll soon get sore.

Some babies need some encouragement to get them to open their mouths wide. Try saying "open" as you open your own mouth; newborn babies can imitate adult facial expressions and learn to associate a word with an action. Your baby will latch on better and nurse more efficiently if you can teach her to take a large portion of the breast all at once, rather than slurping the nipple into a half-open mouth with two or three sucks.

If the baby starts to get upset before she has latched on properly, take a few moments to calm her down. Put her up on your shoulder, rub her back, walk around the room, and when she is ready, try again to put her to the breast. She can't learn what to do if she is crying. You'll find that she's easier to comfort if you catch her before she totally goes to pieces.

If you, too, are becoming very frustrated, get some help—someone to soothe the baby while you take some deep breaths or walk away for a few minutes. Your helper can also arrange pillows for you, get you a glass of water or juice, hold a tiny hand that gets in the way, or help you anticipate just the right moment to pull the baby close to the breast to get her latched on.

Signs of effective sucking

Once the baby is latched on, she will start to suck. The first rapid sucks stimulate your let-down reflex; after the milk lets down, the rhythm will change to slow, even sucks with swallowing after every two or three sucks. Some women feel a tingling sensation in their breasts with the let-down, while others do not. However, the change in the rhythm of the baby's sucking indicates for certain that the reflex is operating.

When the baby is sucking well, you will see her ears (or her temples) wiggle as her lower jaw moves to compress the areola and release the milk. A baby who is latched on and sucking well should not slip off the breast easily. Some babies nurse best if mother is quiet and distractions are kept to a minimum. Others—at least in the first days—may need some encouragement to stick with it. Your voice and your touch can keep baby alert and breastfeeding until her tummy is full.

When to stop

This baby is obviously satisfied and has a full tummy.

Babies can decide for themselves when they're finished nursing or when they're ready to switch to the other breast. Limiting breastfeedings to five or ten or twenty minutes a side does not prevent sore nipples, and it can cause other problems. Let your baby nurse as long as she likes on the first side. When she has had enough she'll let go of the breast on her own.

When your baby comes off the breast, burp her gently. If you place her on your shoulder to burp, her tummy should rest on your shoulder bones to encourage the air to come up. You can also place her in a sitting position to burp, with one hand supporting her chest, neck, and chin and the other patting or rubbing her back. If the bubble comes up in a minute or so, fine; if not, don't worry about it unless your baby seems uncomfortable. Not all babies need to be burped after breastfeeding.

Offer the baby the other breast, and let her nurse as long as she likes—until she lets go of the breast, or drifts off to sleep. If she nurses for only a short time on the second breast, be sure to start the next feeding on this same side.

If your baby falls asleep at the second breast, don't wake her to burp her. In fact, this is a good time to doze off yourself. If you and baby are well supported, snuggled into pillows, you don't need to worry about dropping her. Just enjoy the chance to relax.

If the baby's sucking slows nearly to a stop and she seems to be drifting off to sleep without having nursed long enough (at least five to ten minutes of active

The football hold: The baby is bent at the hips and her feet are up, not pushing against the back of the chair.

The mother's hand controls the back of the baby's head.

sucking, with swallowing, on each breast) you can take her off the breast and use a burping session or a diaper change to rouse her enough to nurse some more.

To release the suction, press down on your breast, slide a clean finger into the baby's mouth, or pull down gently on her chin. Don't "pop" the baby off the breast without breaking the suction first. It will hurt!

Other positions for breastfeeding

The cradle hold described above is not the only way to hold a breastfeeding baby. Sometimes there are reasons for choosing another position—the football (or clutch) hold or the transitional hold.

When using the football hold, again start by making sure that you are comfortable, your back and shoulders well supported by pillows. The baby faces you, and your hand supports her head and neck. Your baby's body is tucked under your arm, to the side, and her bottom rests on pillows that are high enough to bring her up to the level of the breast. Use your other hand to support and offer the breast, waiting for the baby's mouth to open wide and then pulling her head in close. In the football hold, it is easier to see the baby latch on to the breast, and you can provide continuous gentle support on the back of the head to help keep the baby's head in position. Once the baby is latched on and nursing well, you can settle back comfortably into the pillows. If the hand and arm holding the baby begin to get tired, you can slide another pillow or folded receiving blanket underneath for support. Or you can place your foot on a footstool or a low table and use your thigh to prop up your arm.

The transitional hold is useful when babies need extra help latching on. It is similar to the cradle hold, except that your arms exchange jobs. If you are nursing on the left breast, the right arm and hand hold the baby and the left hand supports the breast. Use pillows behind you for comfort and pillows in your lap to bring the baby up to the breast. The baby is turned on her side, tummy-to-tummy with you, and your hand supports the back of her head and neck as she latches on and sucks. As with the football hold, you can apply gentle support to help keep her latched on and nursing. Use a folded blanket or a small pillow under your hand or forearm if they begin to tire.

For some babies, the feeling of mother's hand on the back of the head or mother's fingers near their cheeks is too stimulating. The feel of skin on skin confuses them, and they turn their heads from side to side toward the hand, searching for a nipple. A receiving blanket or a cloth diaper placed between your hand and the baby's head will solve the problem.

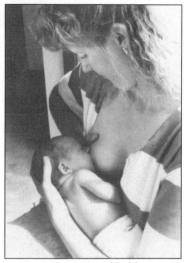

Transitional hold

Breastfeeding while lying down

Nursing while lying down has helped many a tired mother get the rest she needs. It's also a great way to soothe babies off to sleep, or to nurse at night with minimal interruption of your sleep.

You can make yourself comfortable lying on your side with a pillow behind your lower back, pillows under your head, and perhaps a pillow under the knee of your upper leg. Your body is not perpendicular to the bed; instead, you lean back slightly into the pillow behind you. (This is also a comfortable sleeping position for late in pregnancy.)

Your baby is on her side, facing you, mouth at the level of your nipple, and pulled in very close. Your forearm and the crook of your elbow support her back, shoulders, and neck—much as they do in the cradle hold, only lying down. Use your other hand to support and offer the breast, encouraging your baby to open wide and latch on. If you (and your baby) prefer, you can put the baby down on the bed and tuck your arm up under your head, using a folded blanket, towel, or pillow to keep the baby positioned on her side.

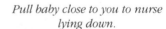

Pull baby close to you to nurse lying down.

To nurse from the other breast, hold the baby on your chest, roll over, and reposition yourself. Or you can continue lying on the same side and roll your body toward the bed to offer the top breast. This second method is more likely to work if your baby is a little older and more adept at latching on.

Some babies catch on to lying-down nursing right from the start; others may need to grow a bit before it works well. Even if you feel awkward at first, keep trying; it's a skill worth mastering.

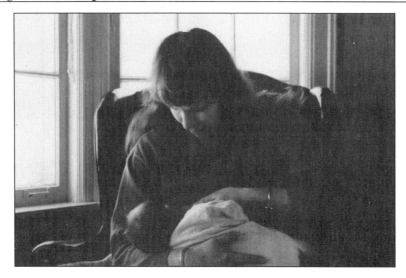

Worrying about getting it right

All these instructions about positioning your baby at the breast can make breastfeeding sound tricky and complicated. As with many other things, it takes a lot more time to explain how to breastfeed your baby than to do it. Putting the baby to the breast quickly becomes second nature for most mothers and babies.

Seeing breastfeeding in action can be a more effective way to learn than reading about what to do. Attending La Leche League meetings gives you an opportunity to observe other breastfeeding mothers and babies. Videos about breastfeeding can also be helpful, although it's best to stick with materials available from breastfeeding advocates, such as La Leche League, rather than free tapes distributed to new mothers from formula companies.

If you and your new baby are experiencing problems getting started at the breast, don't give up—get to work. Most latch-on and sucking problems improve within a few days with patience and persistence. The longer you wait, the longer it can take to teach a baby to nurse efficiently. Use the basic principles described above, and look to the next chapter for further suggestions. Call a La Leche League Leader, or if you're in the hospital, ask to see the lactation consultant or a nurse with experience helping breastfeeding mothers. With a little help, you and your baby will soon work things out.

No bottles, frequent breastfeeding

Most newborns will breastfeed eight to twelve times every twenty-four hours. These feedings will not be at regularly scheduled intervals. If your baby is rooming-in with you, you can offer to nurse her whenever she seems hungry or fretful. You'll soon learn to read her cues, whatever they are—a fist in the mouth, an open mouth searching for a nipple, restlessness, a certain cry.

Newborns breastfeed for lots of reasons besides hunger. Cuddling close to mother's breast and sucking rhythmically help babies get themselves under control when the sights and sounds of the big world threaten to overwhelm them. Go ahead and offer the breast if your baby seems fussy, even if it has been only ten or twenty minutes since she last nursed. Think of it as your baby's dessert. The comfort of breastfeeding and a little more milk may be just what she needs to fall asleep. Many mothers find that breastfeeding for another few minutes is a lot easier than walking the floor with a fussy baby.

Newborns will breastfeed eight to twelve times in twenty-four hours.

Frequent breastfeedings in the early days benefit both mothers and babies. The baby gets lots of colostrum, the first milk that is especially rich in antibodies. Frequent feedings help the baby pass meconium, her first stools, more quickly, which helps to prevent jaundice. These early feedings are also a good opportunity for the baby to master latching-on and sucking before the mother's milk becomes more plentiful and feeding at the breast may be somewhat more challenging. Mothers, too, gain confidence with frequent early breastfeedings; they're reminded of how important they are to their newborns. Frequent breastfeedings bring in the full milk supply sooner and help prevent problems with engorged and painful breasts. Also, nursing helps the uterus return to its pre-pregnant size more quickly.

If your baby is staying in the hospital nursery, ask that she be brought to you whenever she awakens or any time that she cries. Be very specific about asking that she be brought to you during the night for feedings. Tell the nurses that you want to be awakened and that you don't want your baby given bottles "so that mother can get her rest." Taping a "no bottles, no pacifier" sign to the baby's crib informs anyone who might be caring for your baby of your wishes.

Risks of giving bottles and formula

Breastfeeding newborns don't need supplementary bottles of formula or glucose water. Sugar water will not "wash out the jaundice," nor is it needed for preventing hypoglycemia in healthy babies; frequent feedings at the breast will help your baby avoid both of these problems. Supplements interfere with the supply and demand principle that regulates how much milk the mother produces. A baby with a tummy full of artificial formula or water may not be willing to nurse at the breast again for several hours. The mother's body reacts to the lowered demand for breast milk by producing less. If the baby then gets even more supplemental formula or water, the mother's milk supply dwindles still further, and mother and baby are on the road to early weaning.

The artificial nipples screwed onto those bottles can also cause lots of problems with breastfeeding in the early days. It doesn't matter if the nipple's attached to a bottle of formula or water, to a bottle of expressed breast milk, or to a pacifier—sucking on an artificial nipple is different from sucking at the breast. Many babies can become confused if they are asked to learn how to do both at the same time, at least in the beginning. They try to nurse at the breast as if they were sucking at a rubber nipple. It doesn't work, and mother and baby both get very frustrated. Nursing at the breast isn't really harder than feeding from a bottle; studies have shown that bottle-feeding is actually more physiologically stressful than breastfeeding. But breastfeeding does require a certain finesse.

Even if you will be returning to work or want your baby to take an occasional bottle when you are separated, it's better to wait until four to six weeks of age—when the baby has mastered breastfeeding and your milk supply is well established—before introducing an artificial nipple. You may have heard that it can sometimes be difficult to get an older breastfed baby to accept a bottle, but there are ways to overcome this problem, if you should face it in the future. With some very young babies, even one experience with a bottle or pacifier is enough to cause breastfeeding problems that can lead to early weaning.

If your baby does get some bottles in the first few days, for whatever reason, all is not lost. Many babies have no trouble switching from breast to bottle. However, you have no way of knowing before giving that bottle whether or not it will cause problems for your baby. It's better to avoid the risk and get breastfeeding off to a good start. The next chapter has suggestions for what to do about nipple confusion.

Supplemental bottles of formula also carry the risk of allergies. Soy formula as well as cow's milk formula can cause allergic reactions, especially when given to a baby only a day or two old. Your baby's delicate digestive system can be overwhelmed by foreign foods, even if the manufacturing process has "humanized" them. Authentic human milk protects babies' immature immune systems and prepares them gradually for the introduction of other foods.

Engorgement

Overly full, engorged breasts can be a problem in the early days of breastfeeding, as your milk supply adjusts to the baby's demand. Nursing the baby frequently is the best way to relieve engorgement, and get your body tuned in to your baby. Use warm moist washcloths applied to the breast for a few minutes before feedings to help get the milk flowing, and try gentle breast massage as well. Cold compresses (crushed ice in a plastic bag or even a bag of frozen vegetables) will reduce swelling and pain between feedings. Don't put the ice bag directly on the breast; use a cloth or towel to protect the skin. You can also use a pump or try hand expression for a few minutes to soften the breasts when the baby won't nurse or to make it easier for the baby to latch on at the beginning of feedings. While you don't want to stimulate your breasts to produce more milk, it is important to relieve the pressure and prevent the possibility of plugged ducts.

Getting enough?

When you're breastfeeding, it's surprisingly simple to tell if your baby is getting enough milk. True, you can't count the ounces as they're going in, but you can keep track of what's coming out the other end.

Once your milk "comes in," your baby should have five or six wet diapers a day if you're using disposables, or six to eight wet cloth diapers daily. After the black, tarry meconium has been cleared from their system, young breastfed babies will have two to five bowel movements every twenty-four hours; these will be loose and unformed, possibly seedy. They will be yellow to yellow-green or tan in color, with only a mild odor, as long as the baby is getting only human milk. Some babies have small bowel movements after nearly every feeding. In the early weeks, frequent bowel movements are a sign that the baby is getting plenty of the hindmilk, the milk far up in the breast that is released by the let-down reflex. This milk is higher in fat, and it's full of the calories that babies need to grow.

If your baby has plenty of wet diapers and bowel movements, there's no need to worry about whether she is getting enough milk. What comes out must have gone in! After six weeks of age, older breastfed babies' bowel movements may be several days apart, with no signs of constipation.

If your new baby is not having enough wet diapers and bowel movements within a day or two of your milk coming in, you need to take action. Read more about weight gain problems in the next chapter, and call a La Leche League Leader for help with figuring out ways to get your baby to breastfeed better. Most breastfeeding problems improve quickly with a few days of patient, persistent attention.

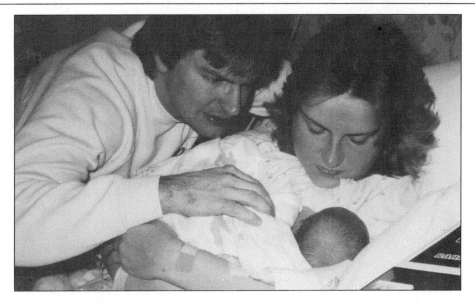

Breastfeeding after a cesarean

Breastfeeding works for mothers who have given birth by cesarean, too. All the same principles apply. Once the placenta is removed from the uterus during the surgery, the hormonal process that stimulates milk production goes to work, and the milk becomes more plentiful within a few days. In the meantime, frequent nursing and lots of contact with your baby will help get breastfeeding off to a good start.

　　Depending on the reasons for the operation, the type of anesthetic used, and the availability of assistance, you may be able to hold and nurse your baby right on the operating table or in the recovery room. Your partner or a nurse can help you position the baby at the breast or just hold and stroke her and talk to her. If you have had regional, rather than general anesthesia, this is a good time to get to know your baby, before the effects of the medication wear off and you begin to feel discomfort. General anesthesia can leave you feeling groggy and disoriented and not yet ready to take in the idea of having a new baby, but as soon as you are feeling alert, ask for your baby to be brought to you to nurse.

Some hospitals routinely provide for early contact between mothers and babies after cesareans; in many others, you will have to ask to see your baby and keep her close. If you know ahead of time that your baby will be born by cesarean, you can plan ahead for these important hours by discussing your needs with your doctor and the hospital staff. If your cesarean is not planned, you or your partner can still request that mother and baby be kept together as much as possible, as long as both are doing well.

Breastfeeding positions after cesarean surgery

Positioning yourself for breastfeeding may take some care in the first day or two after surgery. The side-lying position often works well. Begin with the bed flat and the side railings up. Grasp the railings to help yourself roll carefully onto your side. Besides using pillows to support your head, back, and upper knee, use a small pillow or a folded towel over your abdomen to protect your incision from baby's sudden movements. Your partner or a nurse can help you position the baby and switch sides when it's necessary. After a day or two, you'll be able to hold the baby to your chest and, keeping your feet flat on the bed, turn your hips a little at a time to roll over and move the baby to the other side.

If you prefer to breastfeed sitting up, be sure to place pillows in your lap, to protect your incision as well as to bring the baby up to breast height. The football hold will keep baby off your lap entirely, if that seems necessary.

You'll want to breastfeed your baby frequently, following her cues, with no supplements and no pacifiers. Ask that she be brought to you whenever she awakens or seems hungry or fussy, even at night. Rooming-in is possible after a cesarean, particularly if your partner or another helper can be with you to help with diaper changes and feedings. Hospital personnel can fill in if your helper can't be present all the time.

Medications and complications

Most medications given routinely after cesareans are compatible with breastfeeding. Sometimes a baby born by cesarean may be drowsy in the early days from the anesthetic, from other medications used during labor, or from pain medication given to the mother after birth. This can affect breastfeeding behavior. You may wish to take only the minimum amount of medication you need to stay comfortable, rather than a standard dosage. Some medications are more likely than others to make the baby sleepy or affect her suck. Talk to your doctor or to a nurse if you have concerns about medications or about how your baby is taking the breast.

Women who've had cesareans are more likely to run a low fever in the days after birth. This should not lead to routine separation of mother and baby. Some fevers are the result of swelling in the breast tissue that accompanies the rapid increase in milk production a few days after birth. If the doctor wants to isolate you from other patients because of the possibility of infection, ask that you and the baby be isolated together. Washing your hands before holding your baby will prevent any infection from spreading.

A cesarean delivery may not be the birth you looked forward to during your pregnancy, and you may need time to grieve over what was supposed to have been and to adjust to what actually happened. These feelings of loss or anger can be hard for you and others to acknowledge at the same time that you are rejoicing over your new baby. Find someone with whom you can talk about your feelings—a friend, your partner, perhaps a nurse with a knack for listening. Hospital personnel oryour local La Leche League Leader may be able to refer you to a nearby cesarean support group.

Spend lots of time touching and holding and admiring your baby. These kinds of positive interactions with your baby will help to heal many of the negative feelings that can arise from an unplanned cesarean birth. Go easy on yourself. Each of us is trying hard to do the best she can, but we can't control everything that happens in our lives. Even if you and your baby are separated in the first hours or days after birth, you'll have plenty to time to spend together, breastfeeding and just enjoying one another, in the months to come.

Chapter Four

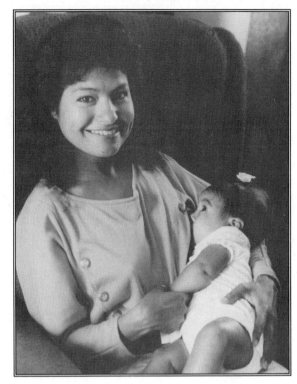

Solving Problems

Difficulties with breastfeeding are not unusual and can have many causes.

Mothers should not blame themselves for problems that occur. Many are the result of a lack of information or poor advice. In other cases, the baby's behavior is part of the problem. It may take time for even a mother who has nursed previous children to learn how best to nurture, understand, and breastfeed this particular baby.

Most breastfeeding problems improve within a day or two. The best solutions are ones that keep mother and baby working together. Temporary weaning or giving supplementary bottles seldom solves the problem that's going on at the breast, but these things do interfere with the mother's milk supply, the baby's sucking skills, and the developing interdependent relationship of mother and nursling.

Don't let breastfeeding problems, which may last only a few days, keep you from enjoying months of nurturing your child at the breast. But don't just endure any difficulties that come your way, hoping things will get better. Figure out what's wrong and why, and take some action to improve the situation. Get help if you need it, from a La Leche League Leader or someone else experienced in helping mothers succeed at breastfeeding. Not only will you solve the problem; in the process, you'll also get to know your baby better and grow to feel more confident as a mother.

Why nipples get sore

The good news is it shouldn't hurt to breastfeed. Nevertheless, many new mothers do experience some nipple soreness in the early days, while they and their babies are working out some of the finer points of latching onto and sucking at the breast. If your nipples are sore, not only will you want to find ways to ease the pain, but you'll also want to try and determine what's causing the discomfort, so that you can fix it and stop dreading the next nursing.

The most frequent cause of sore nipples is the baby not taking enough of the breast tissue into his mouth while nursing. Babies should feed from breasts, not just nipples. They need to take at least an inch of the areola, the pigmented area behind the nipple, as well as the nipple itself. Otherwise, the nipple, with its tender skin and sensitive nerve endings, ends up in the front of the baby's mouth, where his gums and tongue can rub against the same sore spot with every suck.

If the baby takes more of the breast tissue into his mouth, the nipple will end up farther back where it can't get hurt. The baby will also get more milk more easily, as his gums and tongue compress the milk sinuses (the reservoirs where milk is held) that lie directly underneath the areola. You can locate the milk sinuses by trying to express milk by hand from the breast. Cup your hand around your breast with your fingers behind the nipple. Press your hand back in toward your chest while squeezing your fingers together on the breast. When you see milk spurt from the nipple, you'll know you've found the milk sinuses; you'll notice that they are an inch or so behind where your nipples hurt. This is where the baby's gums should be during feedings.

Flat or inverted nipples

Flat or inverted nipples may make it more difficult for some babies to latch on to the breast and take in enough breast tissue to nurse efficiently. Try firming up the nipple by rolling it between your fingers before offering the breast to the baby. Wearing breast shells for twenty to thirty minutes before a feeding will also bring the nipple out. If your nipple seems flat because there is a lot of milk in your breasts, gently hand-express some milk before starting the feeding—just enough to soften the nipple and areola. Flat or inverted nipples can also be drawn out by using a breast pump for a few minutes before trying to get the baby latched on.

Try to stay calm and patient as you work with your baby.

Working toward a better latch-on

Gritting your teeth and putting up with pain during feedings is no solution to latch-on problems. The baby becomes accustomed to doing the wrong thing, and sore areas on nipples quickly turn into painful cracks and blisters.

As you work on improving your baby's latching-on skills, try to stay calm and patient. If the baby doesn't get it right on the first attempt, gently take him off the breast and keep working with him until he latches on correctly. If you and your baby are getting more and more frustrated, stop for a while, wait for everyone to calm down, and come back to it again in fifteen or

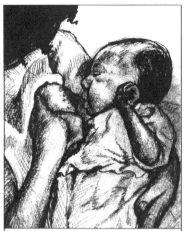

Tickle baby's lips.

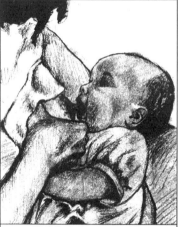

Wait for baby to open wide.

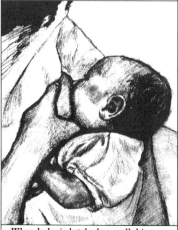

When baby is latched on well, his nose and chin should touch your breast.

twenty minutes. Most babies do catch on within a few days.

Encouraging your baby to latch on better calls for a trip back to the basics. Reread the section on positioning the baby at the breast and latching-on in chapter 3. As you work with your baby, pay careful attention to the following points.

Make sure that you and the baby are well supported, with pillows in your lap and under your elbow all through the feeding; sometimes a baby who has latched on well at the beginning slips down onto the nipple as the feeding goes on and the mother's arm tires. Perhaps you need to be sitting straighter, not leaning back and not hunched over the baby. Remember that you are bringing the baby to the breast, rather than putting the nipple in the baby's mouth as you would with a bottle.

Wait for the baby to open his mouth wide, like a yawn, before pulling him in close to take the breast. Try to anticipate when his mouth will be open the farthest so that it happens just as he takes the breast. Be sure he takes lots of the areola underneath the nipple as well as on top. With some babies, getting that mouth open wide calls for lots of patience. Extending a curved index finger from the hand supporting the breast to firmly push down on the baby's chin can encourage him to open his mouth and keep it open while he latches on and nurses.

The baby's nose and chin should touch the breast as he nurses. If they don't, he has not taken enough of the breast into his mouth. Take him off the breast, and try again.

The baby's lips should be flanged outward. Sometimes a baby sucks his lower lip in as he nurses, and this can cause soreness. If this is the case, you can pull the lip gently outward while the baby sucks, without having to stop the feeding. Also check that the tongue is under the breast, where it belongs, by pulling down gently on the lower lip during nursing. You or a helper should be able to see the tongue resting on the baby's lower gum. If it's not visible, and your nipple hurts, try the latch-on again, making sure that the tongue is down and the baby has opened his mouth very wide as he takes the breast.

Your baby's body should be pulled in close during the entire feeding, his tummy against yours, in both the cradle hold or while nursing lying down. This helps him to stay latched on and suck properly. Be sure to support his head right up at the level of the nipple. Sometimes the football hold or the transitional hold provides better support for babies who need more help in controlling their heads.

When the baby seems overwhelmed by the amount or shape of breast tissue confronting him at the start of a feeding, a technique called the nipple sandwich can make latching-on easier. This is a slightly different way of supporting the breast while latching on. Instead of holding the breast with your hand roundly cupped like a C, flatten the breast tissue somewhat between your thumb above and fingers beneath. The thumb and fingers are the bread of the sandwich, and the nipple and breast tissue in between are the filling. Babies often find it easier to grasp the breast when its shape is compressed like this.

La Leche League Leaders have experience nursing their own babies and can provide the support and information you need.

Call a La Leche League Leader for suggestions about latch-on problems.

Call a La Leche League Leader for support and more suggestions about solving latch-on problems. You may be able to get together with her so that she can see what your baby is doing at the breast and the two of you together can work out what to do about it. A lactation consultant or other medical professional with experience helping breastfeeding mothers may also be able to help you.

Soothing sore nipples

The breasts themselves provide an excellent substance for soothing and healing sore or cracked nipples: human milk. Express a little milk after a feeding, spread it over the nipple and areola, and let it air-dry. The milk's anti-bacterial qualities will help the nipples heal.

Keeping the nipples dry between feedings will hasten healing. Leave the cups of your nursing bra open after feedings to allow air to get at the nipples. Try going braless under a soft cotton t-shirt. If you can't bear to have clothing touching your nipples, breast shells with large air holes worn inside a bra can hold the fabric away from tender skin while allowing air to circulate; in a pinch, rummage through your kitchen drawers and find tea-strainers to do the same job. Avoid bras and nursing pads that are made from synthetic fibers or that contain a layer of plastic.

Many of the creams and ointments sold for the treatment of sore nipples must be removed before feedings since they are not safe for babies. This can hurt and irritate rather than help. Modified lanolin, sold under the name Lansinoh®, is safe to use on nipples during breastfeeding; it is pure and has nothing in it that could affect the baby. It helps the skin retain its inner moisture, which aids in healing. It also prevents cracks or blisters from forming scabs and keeps the skin soft and pliable. To use it, pat your nipples dry after feeding, and apply a small amount to the nipple and areola. Lansinoh® is available from La Leche League International and many local La Leche League Groups.

Breastfeeding while your nipples are sore

Improved positioning and latch-on will usually put an end to sore nipples, but feedings may still be uncomfortable while blistered or cracked nipples heal. Often the most painful part of the feeding is right at the beginning, before the let-down, when the baby is sucking but not getting much milk. Feedings will be easier if you start on the side that is less sore and switch to the more tender side after you notice the baby swallowing more frequently (a sign that the let-down has occurred). If both nipples are very sore, try hand expression or gentle stimulation with a breast pump to trigger the let-down before putting the baby on the breast. Deep breathing and other relaxation techniques from childbirth classes can ease discomfort during the feeding.

Be sure to break the suction before taking the baby off the breast. "Popping" the breast out of the baby's mouth, even just once or twice, can leave nipples hurting for a long time.

Nipple shields, artificial nipples that you place over your own during feedings, are not much help with either sore nipples or latch-on problems. In fact, they usually make things worse. They interfere with the baby learning to latch on and suck correctly, and they decrease the amount of stimulation to the mother's breast, which can affect her milk supply and her let-down reflex. Use of a nipple shield can cause nipple confusion in the same way that other artificial nipples do.

Sore nipples should not go on for days and weeks. Remember, it shouldn't hurt to breastfeed. If your nipples are not improving and feedings are very uncomfortable, get some help in figuring out what's wrong.

Sleepy babies, lazy nursers, and other slow-to-get-started types

Some babies take longer than others in learning to breastfeed effectively. They lose weight in the early days and are slow to regain it. They don't produce six to eight wet cloth diapers (five to six disposables) and two to five bowel movements daily, and hence, don't seem to be getting enough milk. Because of the poor feeding, they are more likely to become jaundiced. Their mothers feel worried and frustrated and don't know what to do. They don't want to give bottles, but breastfeeding does not seem to be working.

There's no need to give up on breastfeeding. These kinds of problems are solvable, often with only a few days of careful attention. It can be hard to muster the will and energy you need to work at breastfeeding during the ups and downs of postpartum adjustments. But if you feel that breastfeeding is important to you and your baby, weeks from now when you have a happy nursing baby, you'll be glad and proud that you made the effort.

Undress a baby down to his diaper to help him stay awake through feedings.

The sleepy baby

Newborns are often sleepy in the first days after birth, and some babies seem to prefer sleeping to nursing. They don't wake up very often for feedings, or they go right back to sleep after only a few minutes or a few sucks at the breast. They don't produce many wet diapers or bowel movements, and may be slow to gain weight, even after the mother's milk has come in. Sleepiness can result from a difficult labor and birth, from medications used during labor, or from another problem, such as jaundice or prematurity.

Don't just sit back and wait for your sleeping beauty to awaken for feedings. Remember that most newborns nurse at least eight to twelve times in twenty-four hours. If he has slept for more than two or three hours during the day, wake him. It's easiest to do if he's in a light sleep cycle—restless, eyes moving under the eyelids, making sucking movements. Talk to him and try to make eye contact. Hold him in an upright position or bend him at the hips into gentle sit-ups on your lap. Change his diaper, rub his back, wipe his face with a cool, damp cloth—anything that seems to stimulate him.

To prevent a baby from drifting off to sleep too soon during a feeding, switch sides as soon as he begins to lose interest in feeding. This technique is called "switch nursing." When he's no longer swallowing after every one or two sucks, take him off the breast, sit him up, burp him, or change his diaper to wake him up. Then offer the other side. When his nursing slows down again, take him off, rouse him, and go back to the first side. Keep switching back and forth for twenty minutes or so before you let him go back into a deep sleep. Be certain that he latches on well and takes the breast far back into his mouth as he nurses.

The lazy nurser

The lazy nurser seems to nurse all the time and yet is never satisfied. He cries when his mother ends a feeding. His lazy nursing style doesn't stimulate the breast enough to produce let-downs during the feeding, and so he doesn't get the richer, higher calorie milk that will make him feel full. He may produce plenty of wet diapers, but few bowel movements. His mother's milk supply may be dwindling because of his ineffective sucking. He is probably losing weight. The lazy nurser uses only his lips to suck. You won't see his jaw moving or his ears wiggling while he nurses. He may nurse almost continuously and protest being taken off the breast.

The switch nursing technique described above will help the lazy nurser learn to suck better. You may have to switch him as often as every thirty or sixty seconds at first, to keep him sucking well and swallowing regularly. Pay close attention to how he latches on.

Sucking problems

Some babies come off the breast easily while nursing. Some don't use their tongues correctly. Some invent other tricks to try during breastfeeding. These kinds of problems may require special help from someone who has experience helping mothers of babies with sucking problems. Many local La Leche League Leaders have had this kind of experience, but if the Leader in your area can't give you the assistance you need, she will know who can. And she will be glad to go on providing support and encouragement while you help your baby learn to breastfeed better.

Pumping and supplementing

Babies who are not breastfeeding well by the third or fourth day postpartum may need more nourishment than they are able to get at the breast. Baby's breastfeeding problems can also cause a decrease in the mother's milk supply.

The answer to both problems is pumping after feedings and giving the pumped milk to the baby. This will help the mother's body continue to produce plenty of milk, and the baby will get the best possible nutrition.

If it seems as though you may be pumping for more than a day or two, renting an electric pump is well worth the money. (Your insurance may even pay for the pump, if your doctor writes orders for it.) The electric pumps available for rental are very efficient, easy to use, and allow you to pump both breasts at once, or even to pump from one side while the baby is nursing on the other. Most hand pumps work very well also, but require more effort from you. You'll need to pump for ten to twenty minutes after each feeding—for as long as the milk is flowing. For more on how to select a pump, how to use it, and how to store the milk, see the section on pumping at the end of this chapter..

The milk you pump after feedings is high in fat and calories, exactly what your baby needs to start growing. Avoid giving it to him in a bottle; artificial nipples usually make breastfeeding problems worse. Even newborn or premature babies can drink milk from a cup. Use a small glass or medicine cup, or better still, a small flexible plastic bowl or cup that can be bent or squeezed to form a spout. Support the baby upright in your lap, with a towel or diaper tucked under his chin, and offer the milk one small sip at a time. You can also use an eyedropper or even a teaspoon to give babies extra milk. Be patient. This can take time, but it really does work. Usually you'll want to give the supplement after the baby nurses. If your baby seems very hungry and irritable, giving him a small amount of milk from the cup before a feeding may settle him down and help him breastfeed better. Experiment and see what works well under which conditions.

Supplemental milk can be given using a cup, eyedropper, or teaspoon.

Supplemental milk can also be given at the breast during feedings using a nursing supplementer. These devices have some advantages, especially with sucking problems that take several weeks to resolve, but they can be tricky to learn to use. For short-term problems, they may not be worth the bother. A La Leche League Leader can help you decide if a supplementer will work for you.

If your milk supply is very low and the amount of milk you pump is not enough for your baby's needs, talk to your doctor about other supplements for your baby.

Even artificial formula can be fed from a cup rather than a bottle. Keep pumping, even if you do need to use a formula supplement for a while; you want to maintain and build up your milk supply so that the milk is there and waiting when the baby's sucking improves.

Pumping and supplementing after feedings take a lot of time. You may finish one feeding, get the pumped milk in the refrigerator and your equipment washed, and discover that your baby's ready to nurse again. For a few days, you may not do much more than feed the baby. It's a good time to take advantage of friends and family who are willing to fix meals, do laundry, and entertain older children. Set up a breastfeeding corner for yourself, with clean diapers, a pitcher of water or juice, comfortable pillows, perhaps something to read—or with the television set nearby.

Nipple confusion

There are health professionals who refuse to believe it, but nipple confusion really does happen. It may strike shortly after the baby comes home from the hospital, and well before the first checkup, so neither nursery nurses nor pediatricians are around to see it. It's the mother who must cope with a baby who had been nursing well but who now acts confused and upset at the breast.

Feeding at the breast is different from an artificial nipple.

Feeding at the breast is different from getting liquid through an artificial nipple. To take the breast, the baby must open his mouth wide; a bottle nipple can be pushed through half-closed lips. The breastfeeding baby uses his gums and his tongue to compress the breast tissue and get the milk out; an artificial nipple requires less participation from the baby. The breastfed baby's lips are flanged out on the breast; with an artificial nipple, the baby purses his lips tightly. Milk flows instantly from a bottle—there's no waiting for the mother's let-down, and when it flows too fast, the baby uses his tongue to block it. This motion, when used at the breast, pushes the mother's nipple right out of the baby's mouth.

One or two bottles are enough to affect some babies' ability to breastfeed. With others, nipple confusion may result from several days of supplemental bottles. In either case, eliminating all artificial nipples is the first step in getting the baby back to breastfeeding. Besides bottle nipples, this means pacifiers and nipple shields, if you have been using them. If your baby has been getting a lot of supplementary formula and your milk supply is low, you'll need to continue giving the supplement using a cup, a bowl, an eyedropper, or a teaspoon. You can also pump after feedings and give your baby this milk as a supplement. You can eliminate the supplement gradually as your baby begins to breastfeed well and his sucking builds up your milk supply. Count the diapers to be sure he's getting enough.

Getting a nipple-confused baby to breastfeed well is largely a matter of patience and persistence. You'll have to work with him as he rediscovers what to do at the breast. Give him lots of skin-to-skin contact and plenty of opportunities for practice. Don't wait for the baby to get very hungry before offering the breast; it's hard for him to learn something new when his mind is on the important business of filling his tummy. Catch him when he's just waking up from a nap, or another time when he's calm. Expressing a little milk onto your nipple may help give him the idea. Encourage him to open his mouth wide by saying "open" and showing him how; even newborns imitate facial expressions. Pay close attention to how he is positioned at the breast and how he latches on. Stimulating your let-down reflex before putting the baby to the breast will assure that his first sucks are well rewarded. Your let-down reflex can be stimulated by expressing some milk, gently rubbing the nipples in a circular motion, taking a warm shower, or even just looking at your baby and smelling his sweet baby smell.

Forceful let-down

Sometimes the milk comes down in such a rush with the let-down that the nursing baby can't keep up with the flow. He may pull away from the nipple or gasp and sputter and swallow a lot of air. He may even start to fuss when put to the breast, because he has come to expect trouble.

Take him off the breast for a minute or so when this happens. The milk flow will slow down, and soon he'll be able to nurse again more easily. You could also position him so that he is nursing "uphill." Use two or three pillows on your lap to raise his head so that he is looking down at the breast while nursing. Leaning way back in a recliner also works well.

A forceful let-down can be caused by an overabundance of milk. If problems like this persist beyond the early weeks, try limiting your baby to one breast at a feeding, at least in the morning and early afternoon when your breasts are more full. If the baby wants to nurse again within the next two hours, offer him the same side he had at the last feeding. For example, use the left breast for feedings between 8 and 10 o'clock, the right breast from 10 till noon, the left breast again from 12 to 2, and so forth. This will help bring your milk supply in line with your baby's needs. Be sure to keep count of wet diapers and stools to be sure that your baby is getting enough milk.

Leaking milk

Leaking milk is a nuisance, but fortunately in most women it is a short-lived problem, limited to the early weeks of breastfeeding. Some women leak milk from one breast while the baby nurses at the other. Others leak when their breasts become overly full between feedings or when the baby's cries or some other stimulus triggers the let-down reflex.

You can stop leaking by applying gentle pressure to the nipples. To do this subtly, fold your arms over your chest and press in. However, leaking is a signal that it's time to breastfeed the baby, and if possible, this is what you should do.

Nursing pads in your bra will absorb the milk. You can buy cloth pads that can be washed and used over and over again, or you can make them from folded handkerchiefs or cloth diapers. Disposable pads with

plastic liners will protect your clothes from wetness. They will also prevent air from getting to your nipples, which can cause soreness, so don't use them all the time. Wear clothing with prints that will camouflage wetness, or bring along a jacket or sweater. If you leak during feedings, a cloth diaper under the breast will catch the overflow.

Newborn jaundice

Jaundice is common in newborn babies, but it is seldom, if ever, a reason to stop breastfeeding, not even for twenty-four hours.

Newborn jaundice is the result of the rapid breakdown of red blood cells in the first days of life. Babies need fewer red blood cells after birth than they did in the womb. As the extra cells are destroyed, a waste product called bilirubin is released into the blood, eventually to be excreted in the baby's stool. When bilirubin is made faster than the baby can eliminate it, the result is jaundice. Bilirubin is a yellow pigment, and an excess of it gives the skin a yellowish cast; the whites of the eyes may also look yellow.

Why does bilirubin reach higher levels in some infants? Sometimes jaundice is the result of blood or liver problems or an infection. More often, jaundice is simply a part of baby's adjustment to life outside mother's body. This kind of jaundice is called physiologic jaundice, because it is part of a normal body process. Physicians disagree about when—or whether—to treat ordinary newborn jaundice; there is no decisive evidence that peak bilirubin levels below 20 to 25 mg/dl are harmful to normal, healthy full-term infants.

To bring down bilirubin levels, babies are placed under special lights, a treatment called phototherapy. The lights help break down the bilirubin so that it can be eliminated more quickly. In extreme cases, blood transfusions may be used to lower bilirubin levels.

The problem with phototherapy is that the baby is out of mother's arms while under the lights. Most likely he's in an isolette in the nursery, with patches over his eyes to protect them from the light. It's hard to watch his cues and breastfeed frequently under these circumstances although frequent feedings are important during phototherapy because the lights can cause dehydration. Newer options in phototherapy include having the lights set up in your hospital room or in your home. There is also a device called a Wallaby phototherapy unit, a fiberoptic blanket that wraps around the baby's trunk, eliminating the need for eye patches and making it possible to hold and nurse the baby while treatment continues. These improvements are kinder to breastfeeding mothers, but phototherapy is still complicated and worrisome to parents. A wise physician will take this into account when advising parents about treatment for jaundice.

Avoiding jaundice problems

Jaundice, bilirubin levels, and phototherapy are not the stuff of which new-baby dreams are made. You can't cuddle and nurse a baby who is under bililights, and it's difficult to be a confident breastfeeding mother if a nurse or doctor is suggesting that your baby needs water or formula supplements to bring the bilirubin levels down.

Good breastfeeding practices work to prevent jaundice.

Fortunately, good breastfeeding practices work to prevent jaundice. Although studies have found a higher incidence of jaundice in breastfed babies, many experts attribute this to hospital routines that make it difficult for mothers to nurse their babies frequently. Colostrum, while small in quantity, has a laxative effect. Frequent feedings right from birth stimulate more frequent stools, which eliminate bilirubin more quickly.

Water supplements do not help to "wash out" the jaundice. In fact, they can make it worse. They fill up the baby's tummy, making him less eager to nurse at the breast. They are usually given with an artificial nipple, which can lead to sucking problems. And water does nothing to encourage stooling—and that's what gets rid of bilirubin. If you have a baby whose bilirubin levels are

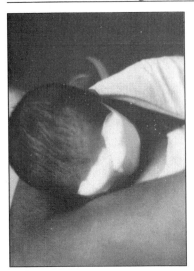

Babies receiving phototherapy still need to breastfeed frequently.

rising, be sure to encourage him to nurse as much as possible. This is easiest to do if the baby is rooming-in with you and stays with you throughout the night. A baby who is not nursing well in the first few days is more likely to have problems with jaundice. Wake him during the day, if necessary, so that he's nursing at least every two hours. Be sure that he is positioned correctly at the breast and that he is sucking actively for five to ten minutes on each side. Call a La Leche League Leader or ask to see the hospital's lactation consultant if you need more help. A day or so of paying close attention to breastfeeding is often all that's needed to turn the situation around and get bilirubin levels to begin to fall.

Indirect sunlight can also help to bring down bilirubin levels. Undress your baby down to his diaper and place him in a warm room that gets plenty of daylight through the windows. Don't put him directly in the path of sunlight coming in the window and don't take your baby outside into the sun; his newborn skin burns easily.

If the baby's doctor wants to begin phototherapy, ask about alternatives. Could treatment be delayed another twelve or twenty-four hours, while you nurse the baby more frequently? By then, a blood test may find that the levels are dropping or at least are no longer rising quickly. If phototherapy is necessary, ask about having the lights in your hospital room, or at home if you are about to be discharged. If the baby must be in the nursery, ask to stay with him there so that you can take him out of the isolette and nurse him as soon as he awakens or whenever he fusses. Phototherapy does not have to be continuous to be effective. If the baby is not nursing well, you need to be able to keep working with him, even during phototherapy. If water supplements are considered necessary, ask that they be given by cup, eyedropper, or syringe, rather than with an artificial nipple.

Some physicians advise mothers to discontinue breastfeeding for a day or two in order to bring down bilirubin levels. This will not really help in cases of physiologic jaundice; breastfeeding more frequently is a better alternative.

There is, however, such a thing as breast milk jaundice, or late-onset jaundice, where something in the mother's milk apparently slows down the baby's elimination of bilirubin. This type of jaundice is much less common than physiologic jaundice. The bilirubin levels do not peak until four or five days after birth, compared to physiologic jaundice in which bilirubin levels are at their highest on the second or third day. Usually, breastfeeding can continue without interruption, though it may take several weeks for the jaundice to clear. Occasionally, when bilirubin levels are very high, the baby with late-onset jaundice may be taken off the breast and given formula (or donor milk from another mother, if available) for twenty-four hours. Bilirubin levels will fall quickly during this time, and the mother can resume nursing. This should be done only in cases of late-onset jaundice and only when the bilirubin levels are very high and continuing to rise. Using a phototherapy unit at home may be an alternative to interrupting breastfeeding.

Jaundice can create a lot of concern for new parents—the treatments along with the condition itself. You need to stay in touch with the baby's doctor, listen to his or her suggestions, and ask about alternatives. If talking to physicians is difficult for you, practice what you will say ahead of time; write down your questions and the points you wish to make. Seek a second opinion if you need to, from a doctor who is more supportive of breastfeeding. Remember that most of the time jaundice is harmless in a full-term, healthy baby, and it should not be allowed to interfere with getting a good start at breastfeeding.

Illness in mother or baby

Colds and flu come and go in nursing mothers and babies, just as in everyone else. You can and should continue to nurse your baby if you become ill. By the time you actually start feeling sick, the baby has already been exposed to the germs, so breastfeeding is certainly not going to make things any worse. In fact, the antibodies that your body makes to fight the germs will appear in your milk and give your baby an edge in dealing with the bug himself. It's not unusual to find that when a cold or the flu rolls through a family, the nursing baby gets only a mild case, if he gets sick at all.

Sometimes a change in the usual nursing pattern is the first indication a mother has that her baby is ill. Stuffy noses make breastfeeding more difficult. Lying on his side to nurse can be painful for a baby with an ear infection. Your baby's behavior at the breast tells you a great deal about how he's feeling, and continuing to breastfeed will help him feel better.

Babies with tummy-aches may want to breastfeed very often—almost continuously. It's okay to let them do so. Frequent short nursings help prevent dehydration, and all the immunities in human milk will help fight the virus that's causing the problems. There's no need to stop breastfeeding, even for a day or two, if your baby has an upset tummy and diarrhea. Studies have shown that breastfed babies with diarrhea recover more quickly and lose less weight if they are allowed to continue to nurse. They will accept the breast far more readily than any other substance offered to them..

Treat a breast infection with rest, heat, gentle massage, and frequent breastfeeding.

A baby who is vomiting may do best with only a little milk at a time; larger amounts may come right back up. In this situation, try nursing the baby on a fairly empty breast. Pump or hand-express for several minutes before feeding the baby. The slower trickle of milk will be more soothing to his stomach, and he'll be able to nurse for comfort without the upset of another episode of vomiting.

Plugged ducts and breast infections

Tender, sore lumps in the breast are usually plugged ducts. A red, hot, swollen area that is painful to the touch may be a breast infection, especially when accompanied by a fever, achiness, and an all-over tired feeling, like flu. Prompt home treatment can prevent a plugged duct from becoming a breast infection and can keep an infection from developing into an abscess. Three things are needed to get the milk flowing again in the affected area: heat, gentle massage, and frequent breastfeeding.

You can apply heat by taking a warm shower, soaking the breast in a basin or bowl of warm water, or using warm, wet washcloths, a hot water bottle, or a heating pad. While it is warm, massage your breast gently with your fingers and palm, using a circular motion first and then kneading gently from high up in the breast behind the sore spot down toward the nipple. Then put the baby to breast or express some milk with a pump or by hand. You may want to continue to massage above the sore area while the baby is nursing in order to loosen the plug and get the milk moving down the duct.

To keep the breast from becoming too full, breastfeed your baby as often as he is willing to nurse, at least every two hours. Use the heat-and-massage routine before feedings, as much as possible, and breastfeed on the sore side first. Take baby to bed with you for a few hours' nap, or just relax with baby in your arms and feet propped up.

Sometimes a breast infection changes the taste of the milk slightly. If your baby is not cooperating and doesn't want to nurse from the sore breast, start him out on the other side. Once the let-down has occurred slide him over to the affected breast, without changing his body position. You may be able to trick him into taking the breast he thinks he doesn't want.

Go to bed and rest if you have a breast infection.

It's very important to continue breastfeeding when you have a plugged duct or a breast infection. Keeping the breast soft and the milk flowing will prevent the development of an abscess, which may have to be surgically drained. Neither pumping nor hand-expressing is as efficient as your baby when it comes to getting milk out of a breast. Even if you had planned to quit breastfeeding soon, keep nursing frequently at this time and delay weaning until the breast infection has cleared up. You don't have to worry about a breast infection making your baby sick. The antibodies in your milk will protect him.

If you are running a fever and are feeling achy, tired, and miserable, go to bed and rest. If you've had the fever for more than twenty-four hours, call your

doctor. He or she may want to prescribe an antibiotic—one that's safe for nursing mothers and babies. Be sure to take the medicine for as long as the doctor suggests. Even if you're feeling better, you need to take the full course of the antibiotic in order to wipe out the infection completely.

Give some thought to what may have caused the plugged duct or the breast infection, so that you can avoid a recurrence. A bra that's too tight or one with ill-fitting underwires can block milk ducts. So can pressing on the breast during feedings or sleeping on your stomach. Skipping feedings, going longer between feedings, or having a baby unexpectedly sleep through the night can cause engorgement, which may lead to plugged ducts or breast infections. Latch-on difficulties can also contribute to problems with breast infections, since a baby who is not latched on well cannot get milk out as efficiently.

Breast infections are often a sign that a mother is too busy or is under a lot of stress. In her rush to get things done, she may delay feedings or cut them short, leading to engorgement, plugged ducts, and breast infections. If she's not getting enough rest, isn't taking the time to eat good foods, or is just plain worn out, her body will be less able to fight off illness. A breast infection warns her to slow down and take better care of herself.

Thrush

Thrush is a yeast infection in the baby's mouth. There may be patches of white on the inside of his lips or cheeks or on his tongue or gums. A mild case of thrush seldom bothers babies, but it can spread to mother's nipples and make them itchy and irritated. Sore nipples that appear after several weeks or months of uneventful breastfeeding may be caused by thrush.

Yeast thrives in places that are dark, warm, and moist—like the mouth. Usually there are other "good" bacteria around that keep yeast from multiplying, but sometimes it gets out of control, especially when people take antibiotics. Antibiotics can kill off good bacteria, along with the harmful kind, allowing thrush to take over.

Thrush can turn the nipple and the part of the areola covered by baby's mouth bright pink. The skin may be flaky and dry. It's possible to have thrush on your nipples even if you can't see any signs of it in baby's mouth. Yeast can also cause a red, raised diaper rash on baby's bottom or a vaginal infection in mother.

Your doctor can give you a prescription for medication that will get rid of thrush—a liquid to squirt in your baby's mouth and a cream to put on your nipples. Diaper rashes and vaginal yeast infections should be treated at the same time. Rinsing your nipples with plain water after feedings may also help.

During the time you have thrush on your nipples, any milk you pump should either be used immediately or discarded. Freezing does not kill yeast organisms, and giving the milk to your baby later could start another round of yeast infections for both of you.

How to express and store your milk

Expressing milk from your breasts, whether by hand or with a pump, is a separate skill from breastfeeding a baby, and it takes practice to become good at it. If you get only a teaspoonful of milk the first time you pump, don't jump to the conclusion that you're not making enough milk for your baby. Your body reacts quite differently to a warm and cuddly infant. With practice, you can get better at pumping, if that's what you need to do.

Equipment

Breast pumps are not glamorous. They're not cute. They're not especially fun to shop for. There may be only two or three kinds of breast pump on the shelf at the local pharmacy or discount store, so you may not have much of a choice there. Other kinds of pumps are available by mail or from local representatives of breast pump companies. (See the resource list in the back of this book for more information.) The type of pump you choose depends on how often you will be using it, how much money you have to spend, and your own preferences.

Many hand-operated breast pumps are very effective, and they sell for less than $30 (in the USA). Some can be adapted for use with fully automatic electric pumps. Most hand pumps require two hands to operate, and your hand or arm may tire while using them. Avoid the cheap, bicycle-horn type; it doesn't work well and the rubber bulb can harbor bacteria.

Electric or battery-operated pumps are more expensive, but they are often preferred by women who are pumping regularly because they've gone back to work. It takes only one hand to use them, leaving the other free for holding a magazine or eating your lunch. Fully automatic electric pumps are very expensive, but they can be rented for several months at a reasonable rate; they're worth looking into if you're going to be doing a lot of pumping or need to pump to keep up a milk supply for a baby who is not yet breastfeeding. Renting a pump is cheaper than buying formula.

Expressing or pumping milk is a skill that takes practice.

Small electric pumps can be purchased for around $100. Battery-operated pumps cost between $35 and $50; they're less effective than the high-quality electric pumps, but many mothers find that they work well. The batteries must be replaced frequently, but many of the pumps can also be used with an AC adapter.

If you're expressing milk for your own healthy baby, you need to sterilize the pump only once—before using it for the first time. Follow the manufacturer's directions for cleaning it, and wash it in hot soapy water after each use. Many pumps can be washed in the dishwasher.

Not every breastfeeding mother needs a breast pump. Some mothers discover that hand-expression works very well for them; it's cheap and convenient, especially for women who don't need to express milk very often. You'll need something to store the milk in. Many mothers use the plastic bags that are designed to be used for bottle-feeding. It's wise to double-bag when using these, as they break easily. Use the holder to keep the bag steady when pouring the pumped milk into it. A more durable plastic bag made especially for storing human milk is available through La Leche League International's Catalogue.

If the milk will be frozen, either glass or hard plastic storage containers can also be used.

How to express milk by hand

Hand-expression is not difficult to learn, but there is a knack to it. Remember that the milk reservoirs are under the areola, behind the nipple. This is where you must apply gentle pressure in order to get the milk out.

A pre-pumping routine will help condition your let-down reflex.

Wash your hands before expressing milk. Place your thumb on top of the breast and your fingers underneath, about an inch to an inch-and-a-half behind the nipple. Don't cup your breast in your hand; instead, the thumb and fingers should be opposite each other with the nipple in between. Push straight back into the chest wall and then roll the thumb and fingers forward as if you were making fingerprints. Repeat this action rhythmically to empty the milk reservoirs. Rotate the hand around the breast and use the other hand as well to reach all the reservoirs. When the flow slows down on one side, switch to the other breast and then back again until you've worked on each side two or three times. Use a wide-mouthed cup or glass to catch the spray.

Avoid squeezing or pulling on the breast; breast tissue is delicate and bruises easily. Be careful not to slide the fingers along the skin as you roll them forward; this can cause skin burns.

Suggestions for pumping

Wash your hands before you pump and have everything you need ready. Moistening your breast with water will create a better seal between the skin and the flange on the pump. Start out at the lowest pressure setting—pumping should not hurt. Pump rhythmically to imitate the way a baby sucks at the breast. Work on one side until the milk flow slows down, then change to the other breast. Switch back and forth until you've pumped each breast two or three times. This should take fifteen to twenty minutes..

But what if you're not getting much milk? The key to pumping or expressing milk successfully is being able to trigger the let-down reflex. A regular place for pumping and a pre-pumping routine will help condition your reflex. Before you start to pump take a few moments to get comfortable and to relax. Close your eyes, take some easy, deep breaths, and think of something pleasant—a mountain stream, a sunny beach. Imagine your baby at your breast and the feel of his skin. If you like, you can gently roll or stroke the nipples with your fingers to help stimulate a let-down.

Massaging your breasts will help you relax before you pump your milk.

Another way to relax before pumping or expressing milk is to massage the breasts. Starting near the armpit, use the fingers to press firmly into the chest wall, using a circular motion. After a few seconds, move to another spot, and repeat the motion. Work around the breast in a spiral until you reach the nipple. Then stroke the breast with a light touch from the top down to the nipple. Lean forward and shake the breasts so that gravity will help release the milk. You can repeat this routine midway through a pumping session to increase the milk flow and stimulate additional let-downs.

When to pump

If you are separated from your baby, you will need to pump about as often as he nurses, at two- to three-hour intervals. If you are expressing milk for an occasional bottle for your baby, try pumping early in the morning, when your baby has not nursed for an hour or two. Most women have more milk early in the day than in the late afternoon or evening. Another strategy is to pump a small amount of milk several times during the day, cool it in the refrigerator, and combine it into one container. If your baby is nearby, try feeding him on one side and pumping or hand-expressing on the other; the baby's nursing will trigger the let-down, and you'll be able to pump more milk.

Storing human milk

The antibacterial factors in your milk help protect it from bacterial contamination during storage. Recent studies have found that it's possible to store human milk in the refrigerator, or even at room temperature, for longer than previously believed. Here are some general guidelines.

Human milk can be kept safely:

- at room temperature for 6 to 10 hours after it is expressed;
- in the refrigerator for up to 5 days;
- in a freezer compartment inside a refrigerator for 2 weeks;
- in a freezer unit with its own door for 3 or 4 months;
- in a deep-freeze at 0 degrees Fahrenheit for 6 months or longer.

Frozen milk that has been thawed can be kept in the refrigerator for up to 9 hours, but it should not be refrozen.

Freeze milk in clean containers that have been washed in hot soapy water. Leave an inch or so of room at the top, since milk expands when frozen. If you want to add freshly expressed milk to already frozen milk, cool it first in the refrigerator and don't add a greater amount than is already in the freezer container. If you're storing milk in plastic bags, stand the bags up in a heavy

There are very few medical reasons why a baby cannot be breastfed.

plastic container with a lid, rather than putting them in the refrigerator or freezer on their own, where they could easily tear.

Human milk should be thawed under running water, first cool and then gradually warmer until the milk is ready for baby. Shake the container before testing the temperature. The milk can also be thawed by placing the container in a pan of water that has been heated on the stove. Human milk should not be heated directly on the stove or in a microwave oven; many of the immunological components can be destroyed if the milk is allowed to get too hot. Uneven heating in a microwave produces "hot spots" that may burn the baby.

As human milk is stored, the fat (or cream) rises to the top, leaving the milk underneath it looking watery or bluish. This is perfectly normal. Cow's milk from the dairy used to do this too, before homogenization was invented. Gently shaking the milk before using it will redistribute the cream.

Special medical situations

There are very few medical reasons why a baby cannot be breastfed. The health benefits of breastfeeding become even more important when mother and baby face special challenges. A mother's desire to breastfeed her baby should be honored, if at all possible, because it is an important part of how she will get to know and feel connected to her child. Breastfeeding matters—for multiple births, for premature infants, for babies with health problems, for mothers who are ill or disabled. Discussing more unusual breastfeeding situations is beyond the scope of this book, but the resource list in the back can direct you to further information. A La Leche League Leader can also help you find out what you need to know and give you the support you need as you learn to breastfeed your baby.

Chapter Five

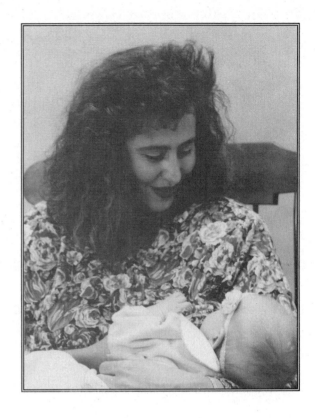

Life with a Breastfed Baby

Babies change their parents' lives forever after—in big ways, of course, and in more mundane matters.

Love, responsibility, concern, pride, uncertainty—these are all a big part of becoming a parent. But you'll also find yourself struggling with issues as basic as getting enough sleep, finding time to eat, and managing to get yourself, the baby, and the diaper bag out of the house with less than two hours of preparation.

Breastfeeding simplifies many of these challenges. It helps build the bond between you and your baby, helps you feel good about yourself as a mother, and provides simple solutions to some practical parenting problems.

Getting enough sleep

From day one of your baby's life and for months afterward, people will ask you, "Does she sleep at night? Is she sleeping through the night? Can you sleep at night?"

This obsession with sleep is well grounded in most people's experience of new parenthood. It's not easy to recover from the physical stresses and strains of pregnancy and childbirth while caring for a vulnerable, demanding infant who knows nothing about the difference between night and day.

Yet a baby who sleeps no more than a few hours at a stretch is doing what is natural and right for her. She needs frequent feedings to keep her tiny tummy comfortable. Frequent—almost constant—contact with mother assures her that she is safe and warm. Being able to wake easily from sleep may even help protect her from Sudden Infant Death Syndrome, which many experts believe is related to an infant's ability to rouse herself when she needs to take a breath during deep sleep.

How can a mother survive? Sleep when the baby sleeps, whenever it is that the baby sleeps. Take a nap during the day. Even if you've never much cared for daytime naps, you may find that lying down and nursing your baby off to sleep lulls you into slumber as well. During the first weeks of your baby's life, housework, kitchen clean-up, and other nagging tasks are not nearly as important as resting both body and mind.

Napping can be difficult if you have other young children. Perhaps mother, baby, and older sibling can all lie down together, or at least enjoy some quiet time with puzzles, books, or conversation. Or bring some favorite toys into your child-proofed bedroom, close the door, and let your toddler play while you and the baby doze. Even stretching out on the floor and letting your toddler tumble over you for fifteen or twenty minutes can recharge your battery and keep you going until bedtime.

Nighttime feedings

New babies do have to be fed at night, and when your baby is breastfed, this is one job that only you can do. Because human milk is digested so quickly, breastfed babies may waken more often than artificially fed infants. One study found that breastfed infants were older before they slept through the night. Nevertheless, it's possible to breastfeed and get enough sleep.

How? Nursing at night requires nothing more than a mother and a baby and a comfortable place for them to be together. There's no trek down to a cold kitchen for bottles, no waiting to warm the formula while baby howls. You don't even need to turn a light on, once the baby can latch on easily. You may not even have to get out of bed, if dad is willing to help out or if baby is already sleeping beside you. You can manage a nighttime breastfeeding without completely waking up, and this makes it much easier to drop back into a sound sleep.

The easiest place to breastfeed at night is in bed, lying down. Once mother gets the baby started, she can doze off, or at least rest while the baby nurses. To switch sides, place the baby on your chest and roll over. (Or, if there's not much room, scoot the baby along the bed underneath you and climb over.) When the feeding is over and baby is again sleeping, you can take her back to her bed or let her sleep next to you until she wakes again to nurse.

You needn't worry about rolling over onto the baby; even while sleeping, mothers are aware of their baby's presence. Pushing the bed against the wall will prevent baby from rolling out, or you might consider purchasing a guard rail—the kind that's made for toddlers who are graduating into a big bed. You and your partner may or may not be comfortable with the idea of sleeping with your baby, but it's worth a try, at least in the early weeks. Mothers and babies have slept together since the human race began, and it is only in the last century, in countries where prosperity has made it possible, that infants have had their own beds in their own rooms, away from their parents. Sleeping together

still works out well for many breastfeeding mothers and babies, enabling everyone in the family to get enough sleep.

It's a good idea to discuss this idea with your partner if you'd like to try it. You'll need his support. A baby in bed with them does not have to come between parents; baby can sleep next to the wall so that her parents can still cuddle up together. And many parents find that keeping their baby with them at night is another way to enjoy this magical being their love has created. One common worry that goes along with a baby in the parents' bed is finding a place and opportunities for making love. If your baby nurses to sleep in your arms, put her down in her crib or bassinet for the first part of the night, while you and your husband enjoy some privacy. When she wakes you can bring her into bed with you for the remainder of the night. Or you can gently move a sleeping infant from your bed into her crib. Remember, too, that beds are not the only place suitable for having sex.

Sleeping with baby isn't for everyone. Some mothers find that a comfortable easy chair, the kind you can curl up in, works well for nighttime feedings. Others prefer a rocking chair. Keep a warm blanket or afghan nearby to wrap around you and baby when it's chilly. Use pillows in your lap to help support the baby, especially if you doze off. Most babies need to be held a few minutes extra, until they're in a sound sleep, before you can put them down without waking them.

Be flexible about nighttime nursing arrangements. They can change as your baby's, your family's, and your own needs change. You can nurse your baby to sleep in the guest bedroom or on a mattress on the floor, and then sneak away to sleep with your husband. This is sometimes easier than trying to put a baby who has fallen asleep in your arms down into a crib without waking her. Older babies can be moved into their own beds after falling asleep somewhere close to you. Dad can help out by being the one who gets up to bring a crying baby into bed with her parents. Try not to count the hours and minutes of interrupted sleep; becoming obsessed with how much sleep you're not getting will only make you feel more tired.

Babies and toddlers who are accustomed to sleeping with parents do eventually "wean" to a crib or their own bed, and babies and children do eventually stop waking up at night. They will do this at their own pace, with some gentle encouragement and guidance from mother and dad. While some contemporary sleep experts maintain that babies must be taught at an early age to fall asleep by themselves, other experts and many parents believe that good sleep habits are best learned gradually, without conflict and crying, as the child is ready, in a safe and secure environment.

And if you do find yourself awake and unable to go back to sleep while your baby is breastfeeding, make the most of it: Think, plan, meditate—or get yourself a rip-roaring, page-turning paperback novel and indulge. You can always nap tomorrow.

Why is your baby crying?

Babies cry for lots of reasons: hunger, discomfort, loneliness, being tired, feeling out of control. What you do about your baby's crying is more important than whether or not you understand exactly what it's all about. Pick her up, cuddle her, walk her, rock her, offer the breast. Change her diaper if she's wet. Swaddle her in a blanket if she's flailing about; she's used to feeling warm and enclosed from her months in the womb. Quiet singing or talking may calm her, or she may prefer gentle jiggling or patting that starts out fast and slows as she settles down. Putting her in a baby carrier (either a front pack or a sling) while you do housework or go for a walk is another way to soothe her. If one thing doesn't work, stay calm and try another.

Babies learn that they can make things happen in the world when someone responds to their cries. They discover that they can trust their own feelings and perceptions, because caregivers take them seriously when they express their needs. As parents help them regain control, babies get into the habit of feeling happy. The more you soothe and carry your baby in the early weeks, the more content she will be later on. Don't be afraid to hold her much of the time. You can't spoil a tiny baby. In fact, "spoiling" her now will make her easier to live with as time goes on.

Don't hesitate to offer to nurse your baby when she's upset. Breastfeeding is a powerful anti-crying agent. The warm skin contact, the familiar feel-good position, and the rhythmic sucking motion will help the baby relax and feel calm again. A baby who sucks for comfort usually doesn't get much milk. If you're worried about over-feeding and spitting up, offer the least-full breast, the one the baby nursed from most recently; the milk flow will be slower.

Some babies cry more than others. Fussy or colicky babies are hard on parents' nerves and on their confidence. It's difficult to feel like a good mother or father when your baby is howling and nothing you do seems to help. But stand by your baby. Even if she goes on crying, she'll have the security of knowing that someone cares about how she feels. Get some support for yourself— talk to the parents of other fussy babies, attend La Leche League meetings, or read one of the books listed in the bibliography about coping with crying and colic.

Babies learn to trust themselves when someone responds to their cries.

"How often should I nurse this baby?"

Newborn babies breastfeed an average of eight to twelve times a day. That's a fact.

But what does this mean for your baby? How do you know when to feed her? How do you know if she's getting enough? Can she really be hungry just forty-five minutes after the last feeding? Why does it seem as though you're nursing all the time?

Breastfeeding works best when it's done "on demand" or "on cue." This means there is no by-the-clock feeding schedule, and mother must learn to read her baby's behavior. This is easier than it sounds, especially if you can let go of preconceived notions (and the instructions in the pamphlet they gave you at the hospital) and get to know your baby as an individual.

Her needs and habits may seem chaotic at first, but after several weeks some kind of pattern will begin to emerge. You and she will both know when she's hungry or when nursing will help to calm her down. In the meantime, go ahead and offer the breast when she fusses or has gone a while without nursing. She'll let you know if she's not interested. "On demand" feeding seldom, if ever, works out to be every three or four hours regularly throughout the day. Babies may learn to sleep longer between feedings at night, but at other times, perhaps in the late afternoon or early evening, they may want to breastfeed very frequently, or be almost continuously attached to the breast. This is normal. Nursing calms frazzled nerves—baby's and mother's.

You'll be spending lots of time nursing your baby in the early weeks.

Some books and some physicians advise that a baby who was last fed less than three hours ago "can't possibly be hungry again" and shouldn't be fed yet. They don't realize that human milk is digested very quickly and baby's tummy may well be feeling empty after ninety minutes or less. In spite of all the trappings of civilization that surround us, human beings are still, biologically speaking, a continuous contact species. This means that infants naturally stay with their mothers and breastfeed frequently, for nourishment and for comfort. If your baby wants to nurse again twenty minutes after the last feeding, go ahead; think of it as the infant equivalent of lingering over coffee and dessert, in the company of someone you love.

Worries about milk supply

In study after study, not having enough milk is the most frequently given reason for stopping breastfeeding. Oddly, this fear has no real basis in fact. The more your baby nurses, the more milk your body will make. Your breasts can make enough milk for twins, or even triplets, if necessary, as long as they receive enough stimulation from nursing.

So why are so many mothers concerned about milk supply? It seems to go with the job. Lives there a mother anywhere who hasn't at some time or another worried about whether her child was eating enough?

Babies also play a part in creating mothers' concerns about milk supply. When babies fuss at the breast, nurse for a long time, or seem to be nursing more frequently, it's easy to assume there's a problem with the amount of milk available. Actually, these behaviors usually have other explanations. Perhaps the mother's milk is not letting down as quickly as the baby would like, perhaps the baby is tired or overstimulated and needs to suck longer in order to unwind, perhaps baby needs some closeness and cuddling to get her through whatever tensions she's noticing in the world around her, or maybe she isn't feeling well.

Growth spurts

One explanation for an increase in babies' breastfeeding time is that the baby is going through a growth spurt. She is nursing more frequently in order to stimulate the mother's breasts to produce the additional milk needed for rapid growth. Growth spurts seem to occur most often around two to three weeks, six weeks, and three months of age. The baby may want to nurse every hour or so for a day or two, but will eventually taper off and go back to her usual feeding pattern. Relax, put other things aside, and let her nurse. Your body knows what to do. The baby's increased demand and time at the breast will soon boost your milk supply, and things will get back to normal.

Things you shouldn't worry about

Your baby's breastfeeding pattern and your body's functioning change over time. Babies become experts at getting milk out of the breast and may shorten some of their feedings while still getting enough milk. As mother's milk production becomes more efficient and in tune with her baby's needs, her breasts may feel softer and less full between feedings, even though they are making the same or even greater amounts of milk. Leaking becomes less of a problem as time goes on, and this, too, has nothing to do with milk supply. Changes in sensations associated with the let-down reflex—or not feeling a let-down at all—are also perfectly normal.

Someone may suggest that you offer your baby a bottle after nursings—"to see if she's still hungry." This proves nothing about whether your baby is getting enough to eat at the breast; some babies will suck on anything offered to them, regardless of hunger. (The breast is ideal for this kind of sucking, since the baby will receive only a small amount of milk when she sucks for comfort and larger amounts when she's truly hungry.)

Don't be discouraged if you try to pump milk and get only a few drops or a teaspoonful. Your body doesn't respond as well to a pump as it does to your baby. Pumping larger amounts of milk is a skill that comes with practice. How much milk you can express has no relation to how much milk your baby gets while nursing.

The bottom line

As long as your baby is wetting six to eight cloth diapers or five to six disposables every twenty-four hours, along with two to five bowel movements daily, you can be assured that she is getting enough milk. After six weeks, as baby's bladder gets bigger, the number of wet diapers may drop a bit, to five or six for cloth or four or five for disposables. Stool patterns may change as baby matures. Some older breastfed babies may go several days or longer between bowel movements, without showing any signs of constipation, or hard, dry stools. When breastfed babies follow this pattern, the once-every-so-many-days bowel movement will be substantial.

With breastfeeding, baby's food comes right from mother's body, which can intensify worries about baby getting enough to eat. These concerns may be connected to how you feel about yourself and your body and to social messages that reach you from friends, family, advertising, and the media. In cultures where everyone breastfeeds and there are no alternatives, the idea of not

Some cultures have never heard of "not having enough milk."

having enough milk for your baby is unheard of. In our culture, where it's assumed that babies eventually will be fed with bottles, every quirk of normal baby behavior gets blamed on breastfeeding.

Weight gain

Just as babies are born in a wide range of sizes, they grow at different rates. As long as your breastfed baby is wetting enough diapers and having regular bowel movements, you can assume that she's growing at the right pace for her. It's impossible to overfeed a breastfed baby.

Slow weight gain in a breastfed baby can sometimes worry mothers and doctors. If everything else checks out okay—wet diapers, enough stools (especially in a baby under six weeks), the baby's general health—she is probably just destined to be a slow gainer, which is fine. Babies don't have to be big to be healthy. Standardized growth charts represent only averages, and the charts currently in use were drawn from populations consisting largely of artificially fed infants. More recent research has found that breastfed babies may gain more slowly than formula-fed infants after the first four months of life. They're destined to be leaner than their bottle-fed counterparts.

Supplementing with formula can lead to the end of breastfeeding.

Supplementing with formula is seldom the answer to weight gain problems, and it can easily lead to the end of breastfeeding. If this is the only kind of advice your doctor is offering, check around and get some better advice. Call a La Leche League Leader; she is committed to helping you continue breastfeeding, if that's what you want to do.

If you have reason to believe that your baby may not be getting enough milk, take a careful look at her nursing pattern. Is she breastfeeding fewer than 8 to 12 times a day? Is she sleeping long stretches during the day without waking up to nurse? Is she nursing only a few minutes at a feeding? Do you hear at least five to ten minutes of swallowing at each breast during every feeding? Is she latched on well and sucking effectively? (For more on this, see chapter 4.)

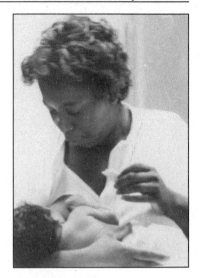

Some simple changes in routine can often improve a baby's weight gain. Offer the breast more frequently. Don't use a pacifier—let all the baby's sucking be at the breast. Switch sides several times a feeding, if necessary, to keep baby awake and encourage her to nurse longer. If she's nursing actively, allow her to finish one side and get all the high-fat milk from that breast before moving her to the other.

A slow-gaining baby can undermine a mother's confidence. It's easy to assume that there must be something wrong with you, and it can be difficult to figure out what to do if you're feeling worried about your baby or down on yourself. If you're concerned about your baby's growth pattern, talk to a La Leche League Leader. She can help you decide if you need to work on improving your baby's breastfeeding habits and give you suggestions about what to do. She can also provide the support you need to feel confident and continue nursing your baby.

Early days at home

The responsibility that comes with a new baby is awesome. And it never goes away, even if the two of you are apart. The tie is especially close when you are the food supply as well as the comforter and caretaker. A new breastfed baby changes life at home and away from home.

Your first weeks postpartum may go by in a blur of feeding, changing, holding, and doing the laundry. Mothering your newborn takes up most of your time and energy. Now is the time to let other things slide, to ask for help from others, and to accept any and all offers from friends and relatives who want to lend a hand— with one exception. Helpers can clean your house, bring you meals, or fold the diapers, but you should be the one who cares for the baby. This is your special time to get to know your baby, and you are the expert on what this baby needs. Sensitive helpers will concentrate on taking care of your needs (and dad's, too), and give you the luxury of worry-free time to know and nurse your newborn.

Unfortunately, postpartum helpers are not always sensitive to mothers' real needs, and the baby's own magic is hard to resist. They'll offer to hold the baby— even give her a bottle, so that you can sleep or make dinner. This is not really helpful to you, and you'll need to be ready with tactful ways to channel their energy into other tasks: "Thanks for the offer, but the baby really needs to be with me right now so she can nurse. Could you take care of something else for me? I would feel so much better if the dishes were done. Then you can hold her while she sleeps so I can take a shower."

This is your special time to get to know your baby.

Showing a new baby off to visitors is part of the fun of having one, but don't fall into the trap of expending all your energy on entertaining, feeding, and cleaning up after guests. Most people are willing to help out, if given some direction. They've been new parents themselves, or at least can recognize that you do need some assistance.

Getting back to normal

The excitement from the birth wears away, your baby begins to grow and change, and the fog of the early weeks lifts. Soon you begin to wonder, will I ever get anything done? When will life get back to normal? Why does breastfeeding seem to take so much time?

Whether you're taking off from work on a short maternity leave or you plan to care for your baby full-time for many months to come, the adjustment to being at home all day is not always easy. During pregnancy you may have imagined yourself cleaning closets, wallpapering the bathroom, or having lots of time for hobbies, while baby napped or looked on from his comfy infant seat. Reality looks quite different, and perhaps the only things you manage to keep up with are daytime television shows that you have plenty of time to watch while the baby nurses.

Life at home with a baby is quite different from going out to a job every day. It is much less predictable, with no built-in schedule, no systematic rewards, no paycheck. Even the simplest of housekeeping tasks can seem daunting when you try to tackle it with a baby cradled in one arm—a baby who has told you in no uncertain terms that she does not want to be put down. Experienced mothers and grandmothers looking back on their baby days are quick to remind you to enjoy your baby while you can, because "they grow up so fast." That may be true, but some days seem endless.

How do you keep all the balls in the air as you juggle household chores, time with your husband and older children, the things you want to do for yourself, and your baby's need for nursing and nurturing? The first thing to do is get your priorities in order: people first, things second. Babies and small children can't wait; adults can, if necessary. Reminding yourself of these two principles makes it much easier to decide what to do first when you know you can't do everything.

The adjustment to being home all day is not always easy.

Second, lower your expectations: simple meals, clean clothes (no ironing), and surroundings that are orderly enough to be safe but far short of the perfection captured in photographs for magazines like *House Beautiful.* There will be time to fuss over these things as your children get older. (Really!) Put away the dust collectors. Open up the meals-in-minutes cookbooks. Get a comb-and-go haircut. Wear clothing made of easy-care fabrics or knits.

Third, think creatively about how to get things done. Anything goes! Cook dinner in the morning before baby wakes up and reheat it when it's time to eat. Make enough for several meals of leftovers. Fold clothes while you talk on the phone. Put the baby in the baby carrier while you straighten up and vacuum. At the very least she'll be content to be near you; if you're lucky, the

movement and the noise will put her to sleep. Invite grandma or another helper over if you've got a really big job to do; she can hold or play with the baby while you work and carry on with the work when you stop to nurse. Set yourself small tasks: clean one kitchen cupboard today, another next week; embroider tiny holiday ornaments, not full-sized samplers; read short stories or try a new magazine, but stay away from 900-page best-sellers.

Be open and honest about your limitations during the time you have small children. Many people, husbands included, don't realize that taking care of a baby all day is a full-time job. Enlist your partner's support as together you work out a lifestyle for your new family.

Overwhelmed by breastfeeding

When you're the mother of a small, totally dependent and very demanding human being, you can temporarily lose sight of yourself, as you are taken over by your baby's needs. This can be a challenging stage of life, and sometimes it looks as though breastfeeding is part of the problem. But if you're thinking about weaning, or giving regular bottles, think again. What do you expect that weaning will do for you? It won't lessen your baby's need to be held, and it won't make her less demanding. It won't decrease her desire to be with you, and it won't make her sleep through the night. In many ways, switching to formula feeding can make life harder, and you'll miss the ease and simplicity of comforting your baby at the breast. Fatigue is common in mothers of infants, no matter how they are feeding their babies.

If you're feeling restless or listless or burned out by motherhood, take a good look at your own needs. What can you do for yourself to help you feel better? Do you need to get out more? Do you need other adults to talk to during the day? Do you need exercise or clothes that flatter your postpartum figure? Do you need more support from your partner or friends? It's not too hard to solve these problems, and paying some attention to yourself will often improve your outlook on mothering and coping with your baby's need for you.

Going out with baby

If you've got places to go and people to see, do it.
Breastfed babies travel easily—just grab some diapers
and go.

But wait! What if your baby needs to breastfeed
while you're out? What do you do then?

Women sometimes hesitate about breastfeeding
away from home, in public places or in the presence of
people outside the immediate family. They've never seen
anyone else do it, or if they have, they may feel that
they're "just not that type." Or their minds keep flashing
back to stories they've heard about nursing mothers
being asked to leave restaurants or department stores.
Such incidents are rare, but they can loom large in the
minds of new mothers.

What is most important here is meeting your
baby's needs. Breastfed babies need to nurse frequently,
and it can be very difficult to bend and squeeze a list of
errands, an afternoon at the park, or an evening out with
your partner into the short span of time between
feedings. Bringing baby along and nursing her wherever
you happen to be makes everything easier. Nurse
discreetly, and you don't have to worry about
disapproving looks. Your baby will be happy and quiet,
and if people do notice, you can take pride in your

decision to give your baby the very best.

Breastfeeding discreetly, so that the breast is not exposed, is a skill that requires the right clothing and some practice. Try it at home in front of a mirror, or ask your partner or friend for a critique. Two-piece outfits where the top is loose and not tucked in to the bottom work best. You can lift the blouse or sweater from the bottom so that the baby can get to the nipple. If the blouse has buttons, unbutton it from the bottom up. The baby covers your midriff, and the top drapes over the breast. Or throw a receiving blanket over the baby's head, your breast, and on up over your shoulder for even better coverage. Sling-type carriers are ideal for discreet nursing; the carrier helps to support the baby and you can pull the fabric up and over the breast while she nurses. A number of mail-order companies sell special fashions for breastfeeding. The clothing—everything from dresses to separates to leotards—has pleats and tucks and openings that are designed to facilitate discreet breastfeeding away from home. (See the appendix for more information.)

Breastfed babies travel so easily. Grab some diapers and go!

Where do you go to nurse the baby at the shopping mall? There are several possibilities. Some restrooms have lounge areas with comfortable seating. These facilities, however, are often used by cigarette smokers, so they're not always the best place for babies, or very pleasant for mothers. If the store is not busy, you may be able to use a dressing room. A comfortable bench along a walkway works well. Or stop at a fast-food restaurant or coffee shop for a drink or a snack, and nurse the baby at a table. The table itself will give you some privacy; you might also want to sit with your back to the rest of the room. (Now is a good time to enjoy meals out in restaurants; it grows more difficult when your baby becomes a toddler.)

Dealing with criticism

Fashions in infant care have gone through many changes in the past century. A generation ago breastfeeding was

out of style, and as a result, many of the people who feel
free to give you baby-rearing advice don't know very
much about it. They may even feel very uncomfortable
with the idea of feeding a baby at the mother's breast.
Their ignorance and defensiveness about breastfeeding
can come out as criticism of you.

Feelings run high when childcare choices are the
topic of debate, and it can be difficult to tolerate criticism
when you're new at mothering and in need of approval.
Sometimes just understanding where the other person's
attitudes and ideas come from will help defuse the
criticism, at least in your own mind. Mothers and
mothers-in-law who decided against breastfeeding thirty
years ago or who tried and had little success may have
complicated feelings about breastfeeding that influence
their comments to you. They may genuinely believe that
breast milk is inadequate or that "women in our family
don't make enough milk." Educating them about
breastfeeding's benefits and how it works may help bring
them around. You can also reassure these critics that you
know they did the very best they could for their babies,
just as you are trying to make your own best judgments
about how to raise your children. Sometimes the only
way to handle critics is to agree to disagree and then
move on to other topics which are easier to discuss.

Sometimes you must reconcile yourself to the fact that these particular people are not ever going to see things your way, and no amount of arguing will change their minds. Of course, these are not the people to go to for a sympathetic ear when your baby is nursing non-stop through a growth spurt or is waking up frequently at night for feedings. When you are having problems with breastfeeding, it's best to take them to someone who understands your desire to continue nursing, even when the going is temporarily tough. If you're encountering a lot of criticism of breastfeeding from family or friends, find out about La Leche League meetings in your area, and attend them. This is one place where you can let your hair down about breastfeeding without having somebody suggest formula as the answer to your problems.

Taking care of yourself

While your baby is small and totally dependent on you, taking care of yourself should be a priority. When you're feeling good, you can do a better job of mothering your baby.

What to eat while breastfeeding

You don't have to eat perfectly balanced meals or follow any complicated dietary rules in order to produce enough good quality milk for your baby. Women all over the world make enough milk for their babies on diets ranging from barely adequate to overindulgent. Human milk quality is remarkably consistent, despite variations in mothers' eating habits. While a steady diet of junk food and sweets isn't good for anyone, it won't seriously affect the nutritional value of your milk.

You will probably find that while you are breastfeeding you can eat a little more than you did before you became pregnant without having to worry about gaining weight. A diet that includes lots of fruits, vegetables, and complex carbohydrates (whole-grain bread and cereals, pasta, rice, and beans) will give you the stamina you need to get through the day. Snack on wholesome healthful foods, and choose water or fruit juice rather than soda pop, cola, or coffee.

Losing weight

You don't have to wait until your baby weans to lose extra pounds put on during (or before) pregnancy. Some women find that they slowly shed weight during the time they're nursing, without even restricting calories, due to the extra energy demands of lactation. Be patient— nursing mothers tend to lose the weight when their babies are three to six months old.

Even if you want to take some initiative to get the weight off—or get it off more quickly, it's not a good idea to go on a quick weight loss diet while breastfeeding. A drastic drop in your energy intake mobilizes your body's fat stores, which can raise the level of environmental contaminants in your milk. Also, you'll be tired and crabby, less able to cope with a demanding infant. Instead, try cutting back on the amount of fat in your diet—skip the butter on toast, use fat-free salad dressing, remove the skin from chicken. Get some exercise daily; put the baby in the carrier or stroller and go out for a thirty-to-forty-minute walk. You can safely and easily lose two or three pounds a month this way, and never feel deprived.

Mothers shed weight while they are nursing without restricting calories.

What not to eat

You don't have to give up chocolate or caffeine or even an occasional glass of wine just because you're breastfeeding. Most nursing mothers can eat whatever they like with no effects on their babies. Warnings about avoiding cabbage, broccoli, chocolate, or other specific foods are merely old wives' tales.

Sometimes, a particular type of food will bother a particular baby, perhaps one with a family history of allergy. A persistent rash or unexplained fussiness may clear up if mother eliminates milk products or eggs or another food from her diet. For more information about breastfeeding and food allergies, see the resource list at the end of this book.

While there is currently some controversy about the effects of alcohol on nursing babies, light-to-moderate drinking—a glass of wine with dinner or an occasional beer—has not been shown to be harmful. Larger amounts of alcohol may interfere with the let-down reflex. Being even slightly intoxicated will affect your ability to tune into your baby and care for her needs.

Illicit drugs and smoking

Smoke from parents' cigarettes is hazardous to babies and children. Studies have shown that children of smokers get more colds and are more likely to have other respiratory problems. You can still breastfeed, even if you smoke, but it's a good idea to cut down. Heavy smoking may affect your milk supply, and your baby may gain weight more slowly. The nicotine from cigarettes does appear in human milk, though the levels are low; if you smoke less than a pack a day, the nicotine will probably not affect your baby. In any case, avoid smoking around the baby.

Breastfeeding mothers should not use recreational drugs such as cocaine or marijuana. Cocaine appears in human milk up to sixty hours after use and can cause cocaine intoxication in the breastfeeding baby. The active ingredient in marijuana, THC, is concentrated in milk, lingers for days after the mother's exposure, and can be found in the baby's urine and stools. As with alcohol intoxication, abusing these and other drugs affects the mother's ability to care for her infant.

Medications

Be sure your doctor knows that you are breastfeeding if he or she prescribes any medication for you. Most medications are safe for nursing mothers and babies, though not all physicians are aware of this—especially those who seldom treat nursing mothers. Sometimes the baby's doctor is more familiar with the effects of medication on a breastfed baby than the doctor who is treating you. If you are being advised to wean your baby in order to take medication, tell your doctor that continuing to breastfeed your baby is very important to you. Often, the doctor may be able to prescribe a different medication, or further investigation reveals that the medication is compatible with breastfeeding. Your local La Leche League Leader can help you find information about specific medications that you can share with your doctor.

Fathers and their feelings

Fathers may have questions about breastfeeding, so it's helpful for mothers to share what they learn with their partners. Knowing about the benefits will help fathers understand that breastfeeding is worth a little extra effort; seeing that it's possible to nurse a baby in a public place without exposing the breast will ease another common worry. Other frequent concerns include whether demand feeding will "spoil" the baby and how breastfeeding will affect the couple's time together and their sexual relations. Talking these problems over as they occur, or even ahead of time, will enable parents to work together so that everyone's needs can be met.

Many men don't realize that fathers are crucial to breastfeeding success. Emotional support from her partner can help a woman grow more confident as a mother and overcome difficulties she may encounter with breastfeeding. It may seem like a little thing to tell someone "I know you can do it" or "You're so important to our baby" or "I'm proud that you're breastfeeding," but heartfelt comments like these make a new mother's heart soar, and she'll remember them for a lifetime. Watching out for the mother's needs while she nurses the baby can be a father's way of showing his love for both wife and child. Arranging pillows, bringing a glass of water or a snack, giving a back rub, playing with an older child, or just sitting and talking quietly while the baby is nursing can help a mother feel loved and loving. Both father and baby will reap the benefits.

Just like mothers, fathers need to spend time getting to know their babies. Even though the mother is doing all the feeding, there are plenty of baby chores left over for fathers who want to get involved. Bathing, burping, walking, soothing, and nuzzling up to a sleeping baby all have their rewards; fathers don't have to give bottles in order to enjoy their offspring. As time goes on and babies' needs expand from care and comfort to stimulation and excitement, fathers become a major source of just plain fun.

Your sex life

Finding the right time for love-making postpartum isn't always easy. Babies consume lots of time and energy, and fatigue tends to dampen sexual desire. Having a baby brings changes to a couple's relationship, and sexual relations may be affected by the adjustments both father and mother are making to new routines and priorities. It's important to talk about these changes and make an effort to keep the romance alive in a relationship. Sex may not be as spontaneous as it once was—you may have to plan ahead, sneak around a bit, and be prepared to take a break if the baby wakes up. But despite these obstacles, postpartum sex can take on a new glow, as the warmth and tenderness parents feel toward their baby spill over into their feelings for each other.

Breastfeeding does affect a woman's sexual response. The same hormone that is responsible for the let-down reflex, oxytocin, is released during arousal, so lactating women may leak milk during sex. Pressing on the nipple may stop the leaking, or keep a towel handy. If you feed the baby or express some milk beforehand you can minimize leaking, if this is a problem for you.

Breastfeeding women may also experience vaginal dryness and discomfort during intercourse. This is related to hormone levels during lactation; it doesn't mean that you're not enjoying your partner's attentions. A longer period of foreplay may help, or try using a lubricant, such as K-Y jelly. Hormone levels may also contribute to decreased desire for sex among some lactating women.

This is only temporary and often improves when the woman's menstrual cycle resumes.

Menstrual cycles and fertility

Breastfeeding suppresses ovulation and menstruation, making it unlikely that a woman will become pregnant again right away. While breastfeeding is not foolproof as a contraceptive, recent research has found a pregnancy rate of only two percent in the first six months postpartum among women who are fully breastfeeding and who are not having periods. This compares favorably to pregnancy rates for many artificial methods of contraception. "Fully breastfeeding" means that the baby receives all, or almost all, of her nourishment at the breast. The baby is fed frequently, including night feedings, rarely gets bottles, and has all her sucking needs met at the breast—no pacifiers.

As your baby starts solids, goes longer between feedings, and sleeps longer at night, the chances of getting pregnant increase, even if your periods have not resumed. Some women ovulate without having a "warning" menstrual period first, especially as the baby gets older, starts solids, or is well on the way to weaning. If your periods have started again, you should consider yourself fertile and take precautions if you don't wish to become pregnant.

Non-hormonal methods of contraception have no effect on breastfeeding; this category includes the diaphragm, cervical cap, condoms, spermicides, the contraceptive sponge, and the copper IUD. The combined oral contraceptive pill may present problems for breastfeeding women; the estrogen component can reduce a mother's milk supply, alter milk composition, and affect infant growth. These effects have not been found with the progestin-only minipill, progestin implants, and injectable forms of progestin. With any type of hormonal contraceptive, small amounts of synthetic hormones appear in the mother's milk, and some experts have expressed concern about possible long-term effects on the baby. You may wish to discuss this with your health-care provider.

Chapter Six

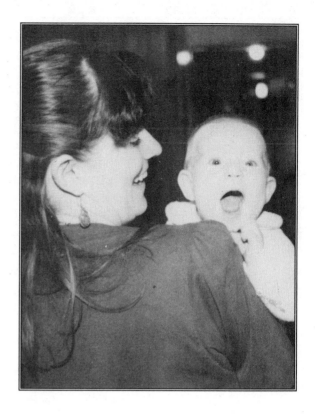

Looking Ahead

Babies change—every day.

Skills replace reflexes, coos and smiles replace the wide-eyed gaze with which newborns once regarded their parents. Growing babies wriggle with anticipation when they know it's time to nurse, and sometimes they stop feeding for just a moment to grin up at mother, as if to say, "Oh, this is *sooo* good." Though mothers may struggle with breastfeeding in the early weeks, they often find that it becomes more rewarding as time goes on— and much easier.

Changing behavior as baby grows

Babies' needs change as they grow. Older breastfed babies may still need to nurse frequently, but not as often as when they were newborns. There will be fussy periods such as late afternoon or early evening, when they seem to nurse all the time, but at other times growing babies may be so involved with playing with daddy, discovering their toes, or watching the shelves go by at the grocery store that they forget about eating, for a little while anyway.

Some babies become so interested in the outside world that it's difficult to get them to settle down and nurse. Feeding them in a quiet, dimly lighted place, at least part of the time, can help, or they may make up for lost time at the breast during the day by breastfeeding more often at night.

Losing interest in nursing?

Babies rarely wean without some help from mother before the age of a year. If a younger baby seems to be losing interest or is refusing to nurse, there may be reasons other than readiness to wean. A stuffy nose makes it difficult to breathe while breastfeeding, so a baby with a cold may fuss at the breast or cut back on feeding time. The doctor may suggest a mild decongestant, or you can use a nasal syringe to clean out mucus from baby's nose. A baby with an ear infection may not want to lie on his side for feedings because it hurts; if you suspect an ear problem, call your doctor. Some babies may change their nursing pattern when they're teething or if their mouths are sore for another reason.

Frequent supplementary bottles are a leading cause of disinterest in breastfeeding. Babies who get bottles regularly may come to prefer them—or at least to expect the breast to act like a bottle. They may complain about having to wait for the mother's let-down to work. As bottles take the place of breastfeedings and the baby nurses less, the mother's milk supply decreases, prompting her to offer more bottles. Soon mother and baby are on the road to weaning, even if this is not what mother had originally intended.

It is possible to build up your milk supply again while gradually cutting out the supplements. The more your baby nurses the more milk you will have. Offer the breast before offering the bottle. Let your baby nurse for comfort even if you don't think he's hungry yet. For a few days, plan on spending much of your time feeding and cuddling, holding and carrying your baby. As your milk supply increases, your baby will take less formula from the bottle, and you can eliminate the bottle feedings one at a time.

If your baby must get bottles regularly because you are working and are separated from him, breastfeeding frequently while you are with him will help keep his interest high. So will skin-to-skin contact and lots of interaction with mother.

Nursing Strike

When a baby who had been breastfeeding well suddenly refuses to nurse at all, it's called a nursing strike. This can be a frustrating, unhappy time for both mother and baby. The reasons for a nursing strike are as individual as the babies involved. You may never know why your baby refuses to nurse, but with persistence and patience on mother's side, most babies will start breastfeeding again in two to four days. Give the baby lots of attention and skin-to-skin contact, so that he remembers how nice it is to be with you. Offer the breast when he's not quite aware that you're trying to feed him—when he's drowsy or just starting to wake up. Try fooling him with a different nursing position. Feed him in a rocking chair or while walking; being in motion may distract him from not wanting to nurse. During the time he's not nursing, you will need to pump or express your milk in order to keep up the supply, and you can give the milk to your baby using a cup.

When a baby goes on a nursing strike or fusses a lot at the breast, it can feel as though he is rejecting you right along with your milk. It's hard not to take it personally. Finding a reason for the refusal to nurse may make it easier to cope with these feelings, but explanations aren't always available. If your baby's breastfeeding behavior has you confused or concerned, call a La Leche League Leader and talk things over with her. She may be able to help you determine what's going on and can give you the support you need in order to figure out what to do.

When your baby gets teeth

Babies can acquire a complete set of teeth—incisors, molars, canines—without their mothers ever feeling a thing during breastfeedings. The tongue covers the lower teeth during sucking; the upper teeth may leave a small mark or indentation where they have been pressed against the mother's soft areola, but this doesn't hurt.

There's no need to quit breastfeeding when your baby gets teeth.

There's no need to quit breastfeeding when your baby gets teeth.

However, some babies do bite, especially when their teeth are new and they're not sure what to do with them. Biting is most likely to occur toward the end of a feeding when the baby is sucking for comfort or playing around.

If your baby clamps down while drifting off to sleep, your main concern is getting your nipple out of his mouth safely. Work your index finger in between his gums and hook it around the nipple as you pull it out; the finger will protect the nipple in case baby clamps down again as he tries to keep the breast in his mouth.

When babies bite for the first time, they can count on a big reaction from you: "Ouch!" This is enough to persuade some not to try it again. Others will go on experimenting. What you do to teach your baby not to bite again depends on his age and his temperament. An older baby may be able to understand that if he bites, mother ends the feeding immediately, and there's no more nursing for a while—perhaps twenty minutes or more. This, along with mother's sudden yell of pain, may be too much for a more sensitive baby to bear, while a younger baby may not be able to understand the relationship between his actions and the consequences.

You can prevent biting from happening by paying close attention to your baby toward the end of the feeding. His behavior at the breast, maybe a certain gleam in the eye, will warn you that he's about to bite, and you can take him off the breast before he has a chance.

Starting solids

Breastfed babies don't need solid foods until sometime around age six months. There are good reasons for waiting this long. Solid foods gradually take the place of milk in the baby's diet. If he fills up on cereal or bananas or carrots, he will not be as hungry and will be less interested in nursing at the breast. As he nurses less, your milk supply will decrease, and your baby may lose interest in nursing sooner than you had planned. Also, solid foods are not as nourishing as your milk. It takes a full and varied diet to supply all the nutrients that children and adults need; a baby's limited intake of solids can not measure up to the complete nutrition available to him in human milk. Thus, early solids replace human milk with less nutritious alternatives.

Early solids replace human milk with less nutritious alternatives.

Allergies are another reason for waiting. Babies are more likely to develop food allergies when they begin solids at an early age. Early solids may also contribute to obesity. Last, but not least, from mothers' point of view, feeding solids to young babies is a messy business. It's much easier when they can sit up on their own and no longer automatically push everything foreign out of their mouth with their tongue.

Why do some advisors, physicians among them, recommend solids even before four months of age? There was a time when babies as young as three or four weeks were fed cereal as a sort of nutritional insurance; physicians were reluctant to have babies depend on only one food product—artificial formula—for all their nutritional needs for a long period of time. This fear does not really apply to breastfed babies who are receiving a completely nourishing diet of mother's milk. Then there's the idea that adding cereal to the diet will help baby sleep through the night. Research studies, along with the experience of many mothers, have shown that this is not true.

Your doctor may suggest you give your baby iron-fortified cereal to prevent anemia. This is not really necessary. Although the amount of iron in human milk is small, it is very well absorbed, and this, together with the iron stores the baby has from birth, is usually sufficient until well past six months of age. If there is any question, a simple blood test can determine if your baby needs an additional source of iron in his diet.

Ready for solids?

Magazine ads and coupons arriving in the mail can make those cute little jars of baby food on the supermarket shelf look very tempting. But it's better to watch your own baby for signs of readiness. You are a better judge of your baby's needs than the companies who are trying to get you to buy their products.

When a baby is truly ready for solids it's hard to stop him from trying them. It becomes challenging to hold him on your lap while you're eating. He grabs for things and is fully capable of dumping your dinner all over the table. He'll watch you eat, following every forkful from plate to mouth with bright attentive eyes. And everything he gets his hands on goes into his mouth.

An increase in appetite is another sign that a baby is ready for solid foods. If a baby who is around six months of age suddenly wants to nurse more frequently, and this goes on for four or five days with no other apparent explanation, he is probably ready for more food. Bring on the solids! If he is much younger than six months, be a little cautious. This change in nursing routine may be just a growth spurt, or the baby may not be feeling well or for some reason may need more of your attention.

Even as your baby begins to eat a wider variety of foods, your milk remains an important part of his diet. It supplies much of the protein and many of the calories and other nutrients he needs each day.

How to begin

A baby's first encounter with solid foods is more like an experiment than a meal. He has a lot to learn about taste, texture, and how to move the food from the front of his mouth to the back and then swallow it. Measure the success of early feedings by how much practice baby gets, not how much food you manage to get into him.

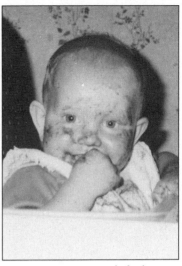

Expect some messes as baby learns to feed himself.

Mashed ripe bananas make an excellent first food; they're sweet and soft and sticky enough to be interesting. You can use fresh bananas right out of the peel; you don't need to depend on jarred baby food for simple, tasty infant meals. If you wait until your baby is about six months old before starting solids, he'll be able to handle a few bumps and lumps. Foods should be soft and mashed, but they don't need to be pureed pudding-smooth or liquefied. Ripe avocado or cooked sweet potatoes also make excellent first foods. Offer only one new food at a time, and wait several days or a week before adding another food. If the baby has an allergic reaction—a rash, diarrhea, upset stomach, stuffy nose—you'll know which food is responsible.

Choose a time when your baby isn't terribly hungry, maybe a half-hour to an hour after he has nursed. Start with a tiny amount of food. (You can increase the portion size gradually as time goes on.) Breastfed babies often feel most comfortable on their mother's lap during these first feedings. You can use a spoon to place the food in your baby's mouth, or try using your finger. You shouldn't have to coax, cajole, or put on a big show to get your baby to eat. If he's not interested, he'll turn his head away, clamp his mouth shut, or spit the food out. Respect his wishes and try again another time. Some breastfed babies aren't much interested in solids until they're seven, eight, or nine months old, and will continue to grow well and stay healthy on breast milk alone.

Preparing nutritious foods for an adventuresome new eater can be a lot of fun. La Leche League's book THE WOMANLY ART OF BREASTFEEDING contains many ideas for fresh, easy foods for growing babies. If you wait until your baby is six months old before you start solids, you'll find that he can soon eat many of the things you prepare for the rest of the family. He may even teach you a thing or two about what's good, and good for you.

Returning to work

Many women continue to breastfeed after they return to jobs outside their homes. They want to maintain the loving feeling of closeness that nursing provides. Even though others may care for the baby and even feed him, only mother can breastfeed; this is a reminder for both mother and baby that their relationship is unique. Reunions at the end of the workday are especially pleasant when the two of you can curl up together on the sofa to nurse and relax before it's time to start dinner or attack the household chores.

The how-to of breastfeeding and working comes down to two issues: how you will keep up your milk supply and how your baby will be fed while you are gone. The way you work these things out will depend on your work and caregiving situations and the age of your baby.

Keeping up your milk supply

Your body will go on making milk while you are away from your baby. If you pump that milk out, your body will make more milk, and the milk you pump can be given to your baby while you're gone. Expressing milk for your baby provides him with the best possible nutrition even when you can't be there to feed him. Pumping will also prevent you from getting plugged ducts or a breast infection.

You'll probably need to pump your breasts every three to four hours while you and your baby are apart. This will depend partly on how often your baby nurses and how soon your breasts begin to feel full. If you're working part-time, four to six hours at a stretch, one pumping session will probably be enough. With an eight-hour work day, you'll need to pump at least twice. Remember to include travel time to and from the job when figuring out how long you'll be away from your baby.

Where to pump can sometimes be a problem. A clean, comfortable private place is nicest; perhaps there's an empty office available, or another empty room with a chair and a lock on the door. Many women have to make do with the bathroom, a toilet stall, or the ladies' lounge, but you may be able to come up with a better alternative with the support of co-workers or your boss. Packing a picture of your baby in the bag with your pump will help your let-down function better no matter where you are.

Pumping requires fifteen to twenty minutes of your lunch time or break. When you're finished pumping you'll probably want to refrigerate the pumped milk or store it in a small cooler. You can take the milk home with you in a cooler at the end of the day, and it can either be given to your baby the next day while you are gone or stored in the freezer for future use. (For help with pumping and guidelines for storing milk, see chapter 4.)

Your co-workers may find the whole idea of pumping milk strange or embarrassing, particularly if you're the first woman at your place of employment to do this. Keep in mind that you're doing this for your baby, and it's important. A sense of humor helps, too. You might even point out to your co-workers that breastfeeding benefits them: your breastfed baby is less likely to get sick, so you are less likely to be absent from the job.

Feeding baby while you're gone

How many bottles and how much milk your baby needs will depend on his age, his feeding habits, and how long you're gone. There are no hard and fast rules. An older baby who can eat solids while away from you might require less; a baby of three or four months who gets nothing but milk may take more. It's a good idea to start pumping at home a few weeks before going back to work. You won't feel as pressured about pumping if there's a supply of milk in the freezer for days when baby's demands are running ahead of what you've supplied. Store the milk in small amounts at first—about two ounces in each container—until you feel more certain about how much milk he'll take at a feeding.

Take the milk to the caregiver's on ice in a cooler. She should store it in the refrigerator (or freezer, if it's already frozen) until feeding time. The baby should get the fresh, refrigerated milk you pumped the day before first and then, if necessary, milk from the freezer. The sitter should warm or thaw the milk gently, holding the bag or container under warm running water.

Many mothers who work continue to breastfeed their babies.

What if the baby won't take the bottle? This is a common worry and occasionally a problem for caregivers. But breastfed babies can be persuaded to take a bottle. Though some people may tell you to introduce bottles early and get the baby accustomed to them right away, it's better to wait until four to six weeks of age, when the baby has mastered nursing at the breast. Giving bottles before that time can lead to nipple confusion, poor nursing at the breast, and early weaning. There's no need to introduce an artificial nipple until about two weeks before you return to work.

Drinking from an artificial nipple is a new skill for your baby, and learning it may require time and patience from caregivers. Someone other than the mother should be offering the bottle; many babies won't accept substitutes when they know the breast is nearby. Don't wait until the baby is desperately hungry to offer the bottle; he's more likely to accept something new when he's relatively calm. Try different positions; some babies like to be held as they would be for breastfeeding while others prefer a totally different posture, facing away from the caregiver or propped against her raised legs. Try different kinds of nipples, with different sized holes.

Hold the bottle nipple near the baby's mouth and allow him to take it rather than pushing it between his lips. Try warming the nipple before offering it to the baby. And remember that even very young babies can take milk from a cup or a spoon, if they decide they will have nothing to do with bottles for the time being.

Making it work

Juggling a job and a baby is not easy. Here are some suggestions that may help you along the way.

During the time you are home with your baby, nurse him frequently. Spend lots of time together cuddling and playing. Put him in the baby carrier while you prepare dinner or do laundry. Nursing frequently while you're together—at night, on weekends—will encourage your body to keep making lots of milk, though you may need to pump more often on Monday or Tuesday to keep up with the increased supply stimulated by nursing on the weekend.

Some babies react to their mother's being gone during the day by staying awake longer in the evening and by waking more often to nurse at night. If you tuck the baby in bed with you, you can still get the rest you need; he'll be able to nurse and enjoy the closeness while you doze. Babies who nurse more frequently at night may sleep more at the caregiver's and need fewer bottles.

Set the alarm fifteen minutes early so that you can breastfeed the baby before you have to get up. This should keep him content while you're getting ready. Then nurse him again once more before you leave.

Choose a caregiver for your baby who understands and supports your desire to continue breastfeeding; your working-and-breastfeeding routine will go more smoothly with this helper's cooperation. Talk to her about breastfeeding's importance for your baby, and tell her what she can do to help you. For example, the caregiver can avoid giving the baby a bottle toward the end of the day, or give only a few ounces of milk, so that your baby is ready to nurse when you arrive.

Some mothers look for childcare near their jobs rather than close to home. They nurse the baby at the caregiver's before going to work and before setting out for home after work. If you have a long commute, this can shorten the length of time you are away from your baby. Sometimes it's possible to go to the caregiver's and nurse the baby on your lunch hour, or even to have the baby brought to you for feedings.

A good breast pump is a worthwhile investment. Many women prefer the ease of using an electric pump; some are battery-operated for use where there are no electrical outlets. It's possible to rent a high-quality electric pump on a long-term basis for a lot less money than it would cost to give your baby formula. These pumps are the most effective at maintaining a milk supply.

Friends may wonder why you "bother" to breastfeed, with all the other demands on your attention. Look to other breastfeeding mothers for support. At La Leche League meetings, you can often meet other women who are combining breastfeeding with employment outside the home.

Supplementing

If you decide that pumping is not for you or that you've pumped long enough, your baby can receive formula supplements when you're not there to nurse him. In babies of four to six months or older, solids can substitute for one or more breastfeedings. You can still continue to breastfeed your baby when you and he are together. Your body will adjust to this new pattern of milk-making, though at first you may need to express some milk while you're at work to relieve fullness. Frequent nursing sessions at home will help keep your baby interested in the breast and remind him that mother is the source of this special food.

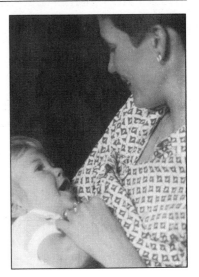

Weaning–or not

How long you breastfeed is up to you and your baby. There's no minimum length of time that you must breastfeed, nor is there a certain age by which a baby must be weaned. A mother can choose to set her own pace for weaning, or she can follow her baby's lead. As long as the baby continues to nurse, the breasts will go on producing nutritious milk that contains valuable immunities.

Weaning is best done gradually, to allow your breasts to adjust to the decreasing demand for milk and to make the change easier on your baby. Stopping breastfeeding "cold turkey" can be very distressing for both mother and baby and can cause plugged ducts or a breast infection. Watch your baby for signs of stress; he'll let you know if weaning is going too quickly for him.

The weaning process begins the first time your baby takes food from a source other than your breast— whether it's formula from a bottle or mashed banana from a spoon. Weaning is the gradual replacement of breastfeeding with other foods and ways of nurturing. Babies who are approaching one year of age and eating a variety of foods may be able to wean directly to a cup; younger babies generally require bottles. Ask your doctor about what kind of nourishment your baby should get in place of your milk.

Eliminate only one nursing session at a time. Offer the bottle or a cup at a time when your baby normally would have nursed. Wait at least two or three days, preferably longer, before you eliminate another feeding. If your breasts feel full from skipping feedings, express a small amount of milk—enough to relieve the pressure and prevent plugged ducts. Within a few days your breasts will be producing less milk and this won't be necessary.

It's easiest to begin by eliminating feeding sessions that are less important to the baby. Be prepared to slow the pace if your baby becomes fussy or clingy, gets ill, or seems to be teething. Naptime, bedtime, and first-thing-in-the-morning feedings are usually the last to go. Take your time with these, especially if you enjoy a bedtime snuggle as much as your baby does.

Weaning sometimes brings feelings of sadness, especially if you have been forced to wean your baby abruptly, for reasons beyond your control. Even for mothers who feel ready for weaning, there may be some sense of loss. Weaning marks the end of a physical oneness with your child, the close of a very special period in your lives. Remember that your baby-child's strong need for your presence continues, even if it is now expressed in other ways.

You can continue to breastfeed as your baby grows.

It's important to be realistic about your expectations for weaning. Stopping breastfeeding does not make mothering any easier or force your child to grow up any faster. Your baby will still demand lots of your attention; supplying this in ways other than nursing can be challenging. Breastfeeding can be a real worksaver when you can count on it as a surefire way of getting a baby to quiet down or sleep. Often there are ways other than total weaning to cope with mothers' feelings of restlessness or being tied down.

If you choose to do so, there's nothing wrong with continuing to breastfeed as your baby grows into toddlerhood. This is the most natural path to follow. Babies who are allowed to wean at their own pace usually continue to nurse well past their first birthday. As they learn to eat other foods and to drink from a cup, breastfeeding becomes more important for comfort and reassurance than for nourishment. These children wean gradually, when they are ready.

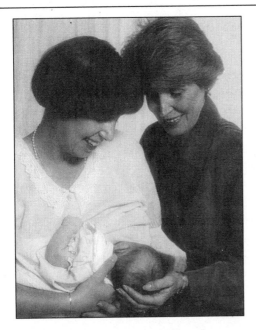

Nursing a toddler is considered unusual in American culture, perhaps because we push our children toward independence at an early age. But in many other cultures around the world, children nurse until two-and-a-half or three years of age or even longer. The idea of breastfeeding a toddler may seem peculiar to you at first; it makes more sense as your baby grows and you see how much nursing means to him.

If you want to know more about natural, baby-led weaning, or about weaning in general, check the resource list in the back of this book, or call a La Leche League Leader. She can help you wean your baby gradually and with love or can give you the support you need if you want to breastfeed longer.

A world of breastfeeding women

Memories of breastfeeding last a lifetime. Studies have shown that women's recall of how long they breastfed is very accurate many years later—a sign of how important a mark nursing a baby has left on their lives. Nourishing a baby at the breast is both profoundly practical and totally astonishing. Enjoy it while it lasts and then treasure the memory as your child grows.

The experience of breastfeeding binds women together, across the barriers of language, culture, and nationality. We can feel a rapport with one another as we seek to give our babies the very best of ourselves. So the next time you see another nursing mother, smile and acknowledge the womanly bond that we all share. Talk about breastfeeding with your friends, join La Leche League, learn about breastfeeding in other parts of the world. If mothers can be more forthright about how wonderful it is to breastfeed and how important it is to babies, we can make this a better world for our children and our grandchildren to come.

Notes

Page 3 Older baby receives greater concentration of immune factors: A.S. Goldman et al, "Immunologic components in human milk during the second year of lactation," *Acta Paediatr Scand* 1983; 722:133-34.

Breastfed babies have fewer illnesses and are less likely to be SIDS victims: A. S. Cunningham et al, "Breastfeeding and health in the 1980s: A global epidemiologic review," *J Pediatr* 1991; 118:659-66.

Each mother's milk protects her baby from whatever is going around: R. E. Kleinman and W. A. Walker, "The enteromammary immune system: an important concept in breast milk host defense," *Digest Dis Sci* 1979; 24:876.

Page 4 Nutritional components of breast milk: For a summary of the literature see the chapter "Biochemistry of human milk," in R. Lawrence, *Breastfeeding: A Guide for the Medical Profession*, 3d ed., (St. Louis: Mosby, 1989).

Enzymes and hormones in human milk: M. Hamosh, "Enzymes in human milk," in *Human Milk in Infant Nutrition and Health*, ed. R. R. Howell et al (Springfield, IL: Charles C. Thomas, 1986); L. A. Ellis and M. F. Picciano, "Milk-borne hormones: regulators of development in neonates," *Adv Exp Med Bio* 1991; 262:69-76.

Page 18 Hospital routines affect breastfeeding success: G. Nylander et al, "Unsupplemented feeding in the maternity ward: positive long-term effects," *Acta Obstet Gynecol Scand* 1991; 70:205-9.

Page 20 Part-time employment and delaying the return to work make breastfeeding easier: K. G. Auerbach and E. Guss, "Maternal employment and breastfeeding: a study of 567 women's experiences," *Am J Dis Child* 1984; 138:958-60.

Page 29 Babies decide for themselves when they have finished a feeding: M. W. Woolridge, "Do changes in pattern of breast usage alter the baby's nutrient intake?" *Lancet* 1990; 336:395-97.

Page 34 Frequent feedings help prevent jaundice and hypoglycemia: D. Tudehope et al, "Breastfeeding practices and severe hyperbilirubinaemia," *J Paediatr Child Health* 1991; 27:240-44; J. M. Hawdon et al, "Patterns of metabolic adaptation for preterm and term infants in the first neonatal week," *Arch Dis Child*, 1992; 67:357-65,

Bottle-feeding is more physiologically stressful than breastfeeding: P. Meier, "Bottle and breast feeding: effects on transcutaneous oxygen pressure and temperature in small preterm infants," *Nurs Res* 1988; 37:36-41.

Page 35 Risk of allergy from supplemental formula: A. Host, "Importance of the first meal on the development of cow's milk allergy and tolerance," *Allergy Proc* 1991; 12:227-32.

Page 42   Sore nipples caused by baby not taking enough breast tissue:
K. B. Frantz, "Techniques for successfully managing nipple problems
and the reluctant nurser in the early postpartum period," in *Human
Milk: Its Biological and Social Value*, ed. S. Freier and A. Eidelman
(Amsterdam: Excerpta Medica, 1980.)

Page 43   Additional material on sore nipples and latch-on and sucking
problems can be found in S. M. Maher, *An Overview of Solutions to B
Breastfeeding and Sucking Problems* (Franklin Park, IL: La Leche League
International, 1988); in N. Mohrbacher and J. Stock, THE
BREASTFEEDING ANSWER BOOK (Franklin Park IL: La Leche League
International, 1991); and in materials by Chele Marmet and Ellen Shell
from the Lactation Institute in Encino, California.

Page 46   Modified lanolin helps skin retain moisture and aids healing:
D. A. Sharp, "Moist wound healing for sore or cracked nipples,"
Breastfeeding Abstracts 1992; 12:19.

Page 54   Physicians disagree about when to treat newborn jaundice: For a
review of the research and treatment recommendations see T. B.
Newman and M. J. Maisels, "Evaluation and treatment of jaundice in the
term newborn: a kinder, gentler approach," *Pediatrics* 1992; 89:809-18.

Page 63   This technique for hand-expressing was developed by Chele
Marmet. For more details, see *Manual Expression of Breast Milk—
Marmet Technique* (Franklin Park, IL: La Leche League
International, 1989).

Page 65   Guidelines for storing human milk: J. Barger and P. Bull, "A
comparison of the bacterial composition of breast milk stored at
room temperature and stored in the refrigerator," *Int J Childbirth
Ed* 1987; 2:29-30; R. Sosa and L. Barness, "Bacterial growth in
refrigerated human milk," *Am J Dis Child* 1987; 141:111-12.

Page 66   Human milk should not be heated in a microwave oven: R.
Quan et al, "Effects of microwave radiation on anti-infective
factors in human milk," *Pediatrics* 1992; 89:667-69.

Page 70   Being able to wake easily related to risk of SIDS: J. McKenna et al,
"Sleep and arousal patterns among co-sleeping mother-infant pairs:
implications for SIDS," *Am J Phys Anthro* 1991; 83:331-47. McKenna
suggests that co-sleeping may protect infants from SIDS events.

Page 71   Breastfed babies were older before they slept through the night:
M. F. Elias et al, "Sleep/wake patterns of breast-fed infants in
the first 2 years of life," *Pediatrics* 1986; 77:322-29; Jeaton-Evans and
A. E. Dugdale, "Sleep patterns of infants in the first year of life,"
Arch Dis Child 1988; 63:647-49.

Page 75   Not having enough milk most frequent reason for stopping
breastfeeding: P. D. Hill, "The enigma of insufficient milk supply,"
MCN 1991; 16:313-15; C. Hillervik-Lindquist, "Studies in perceived breast
milk insufficiency," *Acta Paediatr Scand* 1991; suppl 376:6-27.

Page 78 Breastfed babies gain more slowly after four months: K. Dewey and M. J. Heinig, "Are new growth charts needed for breastfed infants?" *Breastfeeding Abstracts* 1993; 12:35-36; K. G. Dewey et al. "Breastfed infants are leaner than formula- fed infants at one year of age: The DARLING study," *Am J Clin Nutr* 1993; 57:140-45.

Page 86 Human milk quality is remarkably consistent despite variations in mother's eating habits: See "Diet and dietary supplements for the mother and infant" in R. Lawrence, *Breastfeeding: A Guide for the Medical Profession*, 3d ed. (St. Louis: Mosby, 1989).

Page 87 Weight loss in breastfeeding women tends to occur from 3-6 months postpartum. See "Lactation and postpartum weight loss" in M. Heinig et al., *Mechanisms Regulating Lactation and Infant Nutrient Utilization* 1992; 30:397-400.

Page 88 Children of smokers have more respiratory problems: J. Colley and R. Corkhill, "Influence of passive smoking and parental phlegm on pneumonia and bronchitis in early childhood," *Lancet* 1974; 2:1031.

Heavy smoking may affect your milk supply: F. Vio et al., "Smoking during pregnancy and lactation and its effects on breast-milk volume," *Am J Clin Nutr* 1991; 54:1011-16.

Page 89 Most medications are safe for nursing mothers and babies: For an extensive referenced list of drugs compatible with lactation see the statement from the American Academy of Pediatrics Committee on Drugs, "Transfer of drugs and other chemicals into human milk," *Pediatrics* 1989; 84:925.

Page 91 Pregnancy rate of only two percent in the first six months postpartum among women who are fully breastfeeding: K. Kennedy et al., "Consensus statement on the use of breastfeeding as a family planning method," *Contraception* 1989; 39:477-96.

Effects of hormonal methods of contraception on breastfeeding: World Health Organization (WHO) Task Force on Oral Contraceptives, Special Programme of Research, Development, and Research Training in Human Reproduction, "Effects of hormonal contraceptives on breast milk composition and infant growth," *Stud Fam Plann* 1988; 19:361-69; I. S. Fraser, "A review of the use of progestogen-only minipills for contraception during lactation," *Reprod Fertil Dev* 1991; 3:245-54.

Page 107 Women's recall of how long they breastfed is very accurate: L. J. Launer et al., "Maternal recall of infant feeding events is accurate," *J Epidemiol Commun Health* 1992; 46:203-6.

La Leche League International publishes and sells many books and pamphlets on breastfeeding, childbirth, and parenting under normal and exceptional circumstances.

Books and Pamphlets

All of the following materials are available from La Leche League International. Call 1-800-LA LECHE to receive a free Catalogue or place an order using your credit card. You can also call 708-451-1891 or FAX your order to 708-455-0125. Or write to LLLI, P. O. Box 1209, Franklin Park IL 60131- 8209 USA.

Resources

Pregnancy and Childbirth

Methods of Childbirth by Constance Bean (New York: Quill, William Morrow, 1990). An overview of different approaches to childbirth along with information on birth technology.

A Good Birth, A Safe Birth by Diana Korte and Roberta Scaer. (Boston: Harvard Common Press, 1992). How to get the birth you want. Lots of tips on interacting with medical personnel.

Breastfeeding

THE WOMANLY ART OF BREASTFEEDING, 35th Anniversary Edition (Franklin Park, IL: La Leche League International, 1991). LLL's classic, with everything you need to know about nursing your baby.

Bestfeeding: Getting Breastfeeding Right for You by Mary Renfrew, Chloe Fisher, and Suzanne Arms (Berkeley, CA: Celestial Arts, 1990). The basics of breastfeeding with an emphasis on positioning and latch-on techniques.

Eat Well, Lose Weight While Breastfeeding by Ellen Behan (New York: Villard Books, 1992). Nutrition, dieting, and exercise for breastfeeding women.

Baby's First Solid Foods by Debbie Boehle (Franklin Park, IL: La Leche League International, 1993). Pamphlet with ideas for nutritious first foods.

Allergies in Breastfed Babies by Sallie Diamond (Franklin Park, IL: La Leche League International, 1987). Pamphlet on tracking down causes of allergic symptoms.

MOTHERING YOUR NURSING TODDLER by Norma Jane Bumgarner (Franklin Park, IL: La Leche League International, 1982).

The Working Woman's Guide to Breastfeeding by Nancy Dana and Anne Price (Deephaven, MN: Meadowbrook, 1987).

A Mother's Guide to Milk Expression and Breast Pumps by Nicole Bernshaw (Franklin Park, IL: La Leche League International, 1991). Pamphlet with information on types of pumps and how to use them effectively.

Practical Hints for Working and Breastfeeding by La Leche League International (Franklin Park, IL: La Leche League International, 1991).

Staying at Home

What's a Smart Woman Like You Doing at Home? by Linda Burton, Janet Dittmer, and Cheri Loveless (Washington, DC: Acropolis Books, Ltd., 1986).

Staying Home Instead by Christine Davidson (New York: Lexington Books, 1993).

Motherhood Stress by Deborah Shaw Lewis (Dallas: Word Publishing, 1989).

Crying Babies

THE FUSSY BABY by William Sears (Franklin Park, IL: La Leche League International, 1985).

Crying Babies, Sleepless Nights by Sandy Jones (Boston: Harvard Common Press, 1992).

Sleeping with Your Baby

NIGHTTIME PARENTING by William Sears (Franklin Park, IL: La Leche League International, 1985).

The Family Bed by Tine Thevenin (Wayne, NY: Avery Publishing, 1987).

Pumps and Other Equipment

Many kinds of breast pumps, along with breast shells and nursing supplementers, are available from La Leche League International. Call 1-800-LA LECHE to receive a Catalogue. Or call 708-451-1891 to place on order using Visa or MasterCard.

The following companies have electric breast pumps for rent through local representatives, who may also have manual pumps, breast shells, and nursing supplementers available for sale. To find out who to contact in your community write or call:

Amega Egnell Corporation.
765 Industrial Drive
Cary, Illinois 60013 USA
1-800- 323-8750

Egnell-Ameda Medical, Inc.
3 Vista Drive
Fonthill, Ontario Canada L0S 1E2
1-800-665-9533

Medela, Inc.
P. O. Box 660
McHenry, Illinois 60051 USA
1-800-435-8316

Clothes for Breastfeeding Women

The Association for Breastfeeding Fashions
P. O. Box 4378
Sunland, California 91041 USA

Motherwear
Box 114N1
Northampton, Massachusetts 01061 USA
1-800-950-2500

Index

About La Leche League

La Leche League International offers many benefits to breastfeeding mothers and babies. Local La Leche Groups meet monthly in communities all over the world, giving breastfeeding mothers the information they need and the opportunity to learn from one another. La Leche Leaders, women who have nursed their own babies and who have met accreditation requirements, are only a phone call away, they provide accurate information on breastfeeding problems and can lend a sensitive ear to women with common new-mother worries. You don't have to be a La Leche League member to contact a Leader or attend Group meetings. However, members receive added benefits. They receive LLLI's bimonthly magazine, NEW BEGINNINGS, which is filled with breastfeeding information stories from nursing mothers, tips on discipline and common toddler problems, and news about breastfeeding from all over the world. Members also receive a 10% discount on purchases from LLLI's extensive Catalogue of carefully selected books, tapes, pamphlets, and other products for families. Members may also borrow books from local Group libraries. Membership is $30 a year in the USA and helps to support the work of local LLL Groups as well as LLL projects all over the world.

You can pay your dues to the LLL Group in your area or directly to LLLI. For more information on a Group and Leaders near you, call 1-800-LA LECHE.